MAKING MATH CONNECTIONS

Second Edition

*This book is dedicated to all of the teachers who
continue to strive to make mathematics an exciting,
challenging, and sense-making experience for their students.*

MAKING MATH CONNECTIONS

Second Edition

USING REAL-WORLD APPLICATIONS WITH MIDDLE SCHOOL STUDENTS

HOPE MARTIN

CORWIN PRESS
A SAGE Publications Company
Thousand Oaks, California

For information:

Corwin Press
A Sage Publications Company
2455 Teller Road
Thousand Oaks, California 91320
www.corwinpress.com

Sage Publications Ltd.
1 Oliver's Yard
55 City Road
London EC1Y 1SP
United Kingdom

Sage Publications India Pvt. Ltd.
B-42, Panchsheel Enclave
Post Box 4109
New Delhi 110 017 India

Printed in the United States of America.

Library of Congress Cataloging-in-Publication Data

Martin, Hope.
Making math connections : using real-world applications with middle
school students / Hope Martin.— 2nd ed.
      p. cm.
Includes bibliographical references.
ISBN 1-4129-3765-5 (cloth : acid-free paper) — ISBN 1-4129-3766-3
(pbk. : acid-free paper)
    1. Mathematics—Study and teaching (Middle school) 2. Mathematics—Study
and teaching (Middle school)—Activity programs. 3. Curriculum planning. I. Title.
QA135.6.M365 2007
510.71′2—dc22

                                                                    2006004609

This book is printed on acid-free paper.

06   07   08   09   10   10   9   8   7   6   5   4   3   2   1

Acquisitions Editor:	Cathy Hernandez
Editorial Assistant:	Charline Wu
Production Editor:	Jenn Reese
Copy Editor:	Teresa Herlinger
Typesetter:	C&M Digitals (P) Ltd.
Proofreader:	Dennis Webb
Cover Designer:	Michael Dubowe

Contents

Preface

Mathematical things—numbers, statistics, fractals, cyberspace, dimensions, polyhedra, tessellations—have a pervasive way of creeping into our everyday experiences until the objects seem to become household terms. How does this happen? Through comments made by newscasters, statespeople, artists, writers, philosophers, scientists, musicians, architects, people in all areas of life. Why? Because mathematical things help to measure, describe, predict, and quantify so many facets of our lives. Be it things that deal with our bodily functions, our economics, our environment, politics—almost anything you can name will some way have mathematics connected to it. Name ten things you use or do in a day and see how many of these have something mathematical linked to them.

—Theoni Pappas, *The Music of Reason*

The investigations in *Making Math Connections, Second Edition,* have been designed to introduce students in Grades 5 through 8 to the *usefulness* and importance of mathematics in their real lives and how they use math every day. This revised edition is divided into six chapters where connections are made between mathematics and science, social studies, literature, and art. These chapters are: "Our Earth: Natural Disasters," "Physics, Formulas, and Math," "Our Body Systems, Forensics, and Math," "Quilts, Tessellations, and Three-Dimensional Geometry," "The Stock Market Project," and "Math and Literature." The chapters are not organized by mathematics scope and sequence but rather by topics, and are designed to teach important middle school math skills and concepts through real-world applications—showing students that school math and real math are not mutually exclusive. Why is this approach so important?

I once asked a group of seventh-grade students, "Do you think that your answer makes sense?" Without blinking an eye, one of the students answered, "Math hasn't made sense since fifth grade! We just memorize how to get the answers and you know, the way to get the right answer doesn't *always* make sense!" How could *my* students believe that "math made no sense"? And, more important, how could I make mathematics a sense-making experience for them?

Research shows that children do not enter school believing mathematics to be irrelevant to their everyday lives. The National Research Council (2001) states that children actually begin learning mathematics well before they enter school. Many of their experiences require them to use mathematics in a "real-world" setting. They share equally, count their toys, judge who has the most or the least, and "calculate" how many more marbles they need to get to a particular number. These children do not perceive mathematics as an isolated subject with rules and procedures, but as a useful and efficient way to quantify and understand their world.

However, when students enter a classroom where the primary focus is the memorization of arithmetic facts, where there is a preoccupation with learning rote and low-level computational skills, children may lose their belief that mathematics "makes sense." They become passive recipients of isolated rules rather than active participants in connected learning. Mathematics is no longer a tool to help them problem-solve. "School math" and "real math" become disconnected; students' curiosity and interest decline. How can we maintain the students' belief that mathematics is important—a vital and meaningful tool that we use to help us interpret and quantify our modern world? They need to see the relationship between what they are learning and their lives outside of the mathematics classroom.

One current theory of mathematics education, Realistic Mathematics Education (RME), maintains that mathematics is a *human activity* and must be connected to reality (Freudenthal, 1991). This teaching and learning theory of mathematics education, introduced in the Netherlands at the Freudenthal Institute (Zulkardi & Nieveen, 2001), has five components: (1) using a real-world context as a starting point for learning, (2) using visual models to bridge the gap between abstract and applied mathematics, (3) having students develop their own problem-solving strategies for "doing" mathematics, (4) making mathematical communication an integral part of the lesson, and (5) connecting mathematics to other disciplines and to meaningful real-world problems. *School mathematics* becomes connected to *real mathematics* when students understand how it opens doors to future careers. When teachers emphasize mathematical connections, they help students see mathematics as an integrated whole rather than as a set of isolated and disconnected skills and procedures that are to be learned by rote memorization. It is through mathematical applications that students perceive the *usefulness* of mathematics and appreciate the need to study and understand mathematical skills and concepts.

The chart on page xiv illustrates how each activity can be aligned with the mathematics curriculum. The National Council of Teachers of Mathematics' *Principles and Standards of School Mathematics* (NCTM, 2000) has divided 10 standards into two groups: the Content Standards and the Process Standards. The five Content Standards—Number and Operation, Algebra, Geometry, Measurement, and Data Analysis and Probability—clearly describe the content that students should learn. The five Process Standards—Problem Solving, Reasoning and Proof, Communication, Connections, and Representation—illustrate what students should be doing to acquire and use the content knowledge. "This set of ten Standards does not neatly separate the school mathematics curriculum into nonintersecting subsets. . . . Process can be learned within the Content Standards and content can be learned within the Process Standards. Rich connections and intersections abound" (NCTM, 2000, pp. 30–31).

The activities and projects in *Making Math Connections* concentrate on mathematical applications and making mathematical connections. The "Connection" Standard, one of the Process Standards, states that

Instructional programs . . . should enable students to—

- recognize and use connections among mathematical ideas;
- understand how mathematical ideas interconnect and build on one another to produce a coherent whole;
- recognize and apply mathematics in contexts outside of mathematics.

—NCTM, 2000 (p. 64)

HOW IS THE BOOK ORGANIZED?

The activities in *Making Math Connections* were designed for use in mathematics class, Grades 5 through 8. Each of the chapters is organized in the following manner:

I. The Venn Diagram visually describes the interrelationship between curricular areas. These diagrams are included to help middle school instructional teams work together to plan integrated units and to help mathematics teachers relate the activities to real-world applications. Following the Venn diagrams is a brief introduction of the chapter with descriptions of each of the activities.

II. Teacher's Planning Information: There are several pages of planning information for each activity. These pages contain the following:

1. *Mathematical Connections:* Principal mathematical skills and concepts are listed. These mathematically rich problems make connections to a variety of Content and Process Standards and therefore correlate to more than one math skill.

2. *Other Curricular Connections:* A brief description of the curricular interrelationships of the lesson.

3. *Concepts:* The mathematical concepts are delineated in terms of student outcomes. A careful analysis of these concepts will help define the assessment components to develop teacher-designed rubrics.

4. *Materials Needed:* Before beginning the investigation, carefully check out the list of required materials.

5. *Background Information and Procedures:* This area has been expanded in this second edition. Since the activities relate to subject areas other than mathematics, background information has been supplied to the mathematics teacher to help explain how the activity connects to other disciplines. For example, what criteria do scientists use to compare the intensity or magnitude of natural disasters? The Teacher's Planning Information for "Our Earth: Natural Disasters" contains historical

information and tables that describe the scales used to measure earthquakes, volcanoes, hurricanes, and tornadoes. Procedures include a brief outline of the activity—not a detailed, step-by-step analysis of the lesson. This section contains suggestions for introducing the lesson through the use of questioning and student discussion. It is important for students to "buy into" the lesson and be curious about the final results.

6. *Assessment:*
   (a) Most of the activities have student worksheets that require calculations and problem solving. These can be used as part of the assessment process.
   (b) Each activity includes at least one journal question that gives students the opportunity to communicate mathematically by either describing the activity in their own words or applying what they learned to a new problem. Answers have been included for those journal questions that require computation.
   (c) Teacher-designed rubrics can also be used to assess other aspects of the activity.

7. *Selected Answers:* When a lesson has a unique answer, it will be found at the end of the Teacher's Planning Information for that lesson rather than at the back of the book (as in the first edition).

III. The Math Investigation: Following the teacher's planning pages are ready-to-use activities. Fourteen of these investigations are new to the second edition. These include activities related to poetry and other literature, forensic science, and symmetry. In addition, data for all of the activities has been updated to make them more current. While the investigations are very different, their purpose is to encourage students to participate in mathematical applications and they encourage active student involvement. Many times students work collaboratively to problem-solve solutions.

IV. Additional Readings and Internet Web Sites: At the end of each chapter there are suggestions of books that relate to the activities in the entire chapter. These are books that students might enjoy or the teacher can use to obtain ideas for additional activities. A brief description of each book is included. If there are related Web sites, they are included in this section as well. These provide additional resources and data for both teacher and student use.

In addition, the Resources section at the back of the book includes material to help teachers plan their middle school mathematics lessons:

Resource A: "Alternatives to Traditional Assessment" is a discussion of alternatives to traditional assessment strategies. Not all activities can be graded as "right" or "wrong"—a more multifaceted assessment is required.

Resource B: "Design Your Own Lessons" contains suggestions to help with planning and blank forms to organize your ideas.

Acknowledgments

Corwin Press gratefully acknowledges the contributions of the following reviewers:

Erin Beers, Sixth-Grade Teacher
Allison Elementary School, Norwood, OH

Joan Commons, Coordinator of the Elementary Math and Science Institute
University of California, San Diego, CA

Cindy Gulisano, Fifth-Grade Teacher
Lingle/Fort Laramie Elementary School, Lingle, WY

JoAnn Hiatt, Mathematics Teacher
Olathe East High School, Olathe, KS

Steven Isaak, Mathematics Teacher
Advanced Technologies Academy, Las Vegas, NV

Natalie Jakucyn, Mathematics Teacher
Glenbrook South High School, Glenview, IL

Julia Koble, Tenth-Grade Science Teacher
Minot High School, Minot, ND

Felicia M. Moore, Assistant Professor of Science Education
Teachers College, New York, NY

Melinda Day Webster, Third-Grade Teacher
Lenoir City Elementary School, Lenoir City, TN

About the Author

 **Hope Martin** is an innovative mathematics teacher with over 40 years of experience. Having worked with children in elementary, middle, and high school and with teachers in local universities, she is currently a private educational consultant facilitating workshops in the United States, Canada, and Iceland. Her spoon collection confirms her visits to 42 states, two Canadian provinces, and one country that spans both North America and Europe—Iceland is the site of part of the Mid-Atlantic Ridge, where the North American plate is pulling away from the European plate. So Iceland lies both in North America and Europe!

Hope was born and raised in the Bronx, New York, receiving her Bachelor's degree from Brooklyn College. She began her teaching career in Skokie, Illinois, and helped design the mathematics program related to the "New Math" that gained popularity during the 1960s. She left the classroom for 8 years—raising her three children and obtaining her Master's Degree in Mathematics Education from Northeastern Illinois University.

Returning to teaching in 1973, Hope saw a drastic change in the educational climate. Schools were now teaching a "back to the basics" curriculum. The "math pendulum" continues to swing back and forth between innovative and traditional philosophies. However, Hope's personal experiences and knowledge of educational learning theories has convinced her that students learn mathematics more effectively when they are active participants and see its relevance to their own lives. Learning math must be a sense-making experience for effective learning to take place!

Hope lives with her husband, Arnie, in Buffalo Grove, Illinois. Arnie is a musician who helps her with her math songs. She has three grown children, Wendy, Shawn, and Lynne; a daughter-in-law, Jill; and two grandchildren, 8-year-old Joshua and 5-year-old Stephanie. She is thrilled that they all live within 3 miles of each other.

Alignment With NCTM Standards

Exploration	Content Standards					Process Standards				
	Number & Operation	Algebra	Geometry	Measurement	Data Analysis & Probability	Problem Solving	Reasoning & Proof	Communication	Connections	Representation
Our Earth: Natural Disasters										
Earthquakes	•	•	•	•	•	•	•	•	•	•
Volcanoes	•			•	•	•		•	•	
Hurricanes	•	•	•	•	•	•		•	•	•
Tornadoes	•	•		•		•	•	•	•	•
Physics, Formulas, and Math										
Sports Balls and Density	•		•	•		•		•	•	•
Swings of the Pendulum	•		•	•		•		•	•	
Roller Coasters: How Fast Are We Falling?	•	•				•	•	•	•	•
Our Body Systems, Forensics, and Math										
Our Remarkable Heart	•		•	•	•	•		•	•	•
The Sum of the Parts: How Long Is Your Digestive System?	•			•	•	•		•	•	
Find Your Body's Ratios	•			•	•	•		•	•	•
Forensics and the Human Skeleton	•	•		•	•	•		•	•	
Fingerprints: A Unique Classification	•	•		•	•	•		•	•	•
Quilts, Tessellations, and Three-Dimensional Geometry										
The Geometry of Quilts										
Mathematics and the Snails Trails Quilt Block	•		•			•		•	•	
Designing a Symmetrical Quilt			•			•		•	•	
The Hawaiian Quilt Square			•	•		•		•	•	
Semi-Regular Tessellations: Designs and Angles	•	•			•	•	•	•	•	
Platonic Solids: Designs in Three Dimensions		•	•	•		•		•	•	
The Stock Market Project	•				•	•		•	•	•

Exploration	Content Standards					Process Standards				
	Number & Operation	Algebra	Geometry	Measurement	Data Analysis & Probability	Problem Solving	Reasoning & Proof	Communication	Connections	Representation
Math and Literature										
Looking for Math in Poetry										
Capture-Recapture: How Many Beans?	●					●			●	●
Flavors of Ice Cream	●	●			●	●		●	●	
Overdue Book Fines	●					●			●	
Traveling to Lilliput: How Little Were the Lilliputians?	●			●	●	●		●	●	●
A Million Is a Very Big Number										
Spending $1,000,000	●	●				●		●	●	
How Big a Box Do We Need for 1,000,000 Pennies?	●					●		●	●	
A Million Stars	●		●	●		●		●	●	

Our Earth: Natural Disasters 1

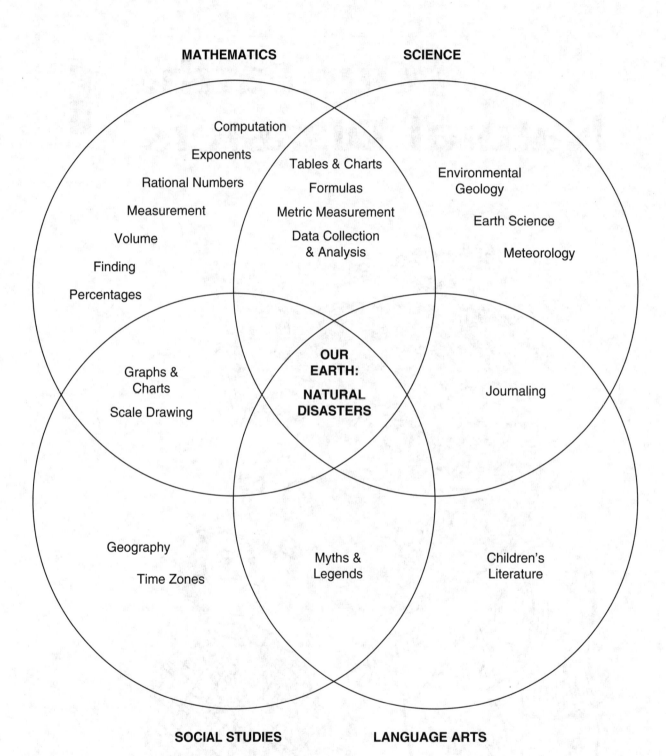

MATHEMATICS

SCIENCE

Computation

Exponents

Rational Numbers

Measurement

Volume

Finding

Percentages

Tables & Charts

Formulas

Metric Measurement

Data Collection
& Analysis

Environmental
Geology

Earth Science

Meteorology

Graphs &
Charts

Scale Drawing

**OUR
EARTH:**

**NATURAL
DISASTERS**

Journaling

Geography

Time Zones

Myths &
Legends

Children's
Literature

SOCIAL STUDIES

LANGUAGE ARTS

Our Earth: 1
Natural Disasters

The profound study of nature is the most fertile source of mathematical discoveries.

—Joseph Fourier

INTRODUCTION

The study of natural disasters extends across the disciplines. Their enormous power is awesome. We are all fascinated with such destructive natural forces, and this topic has built-in motivation for middle school youngsters. This chapter is subdivided into four powerful forces of nature: earthquakes, volcanoes, hurricanes, and tornadoes.

The first section examines some of the major earthquakes that have occurred throughout history. The myths and legends surrounding earthquakes date back thousands of years. According to Hindu mythology, earthquakes occurred when one of the eight elephants that carried the Earth on their backs became tired. Japanese legend blamed earthquakes on a giant catfish, the Namazu, which lived beneath the mud. These tales form a fascinating collection of stories for students. Additional literature related to the myths and legends of earthquakes can be found in the "Additional Reading" section at the end of the chapter.

The second section examines volcanoes and their destructive power. There are over 600 active volcanoes on Earth. More than half of them are found in the same area where the most powerful earthquakes occur—in the so-called "Ring of Fire." The myths and legends surrounding volcanoes are even more far-reaching than those about earthquakes. Primitive tribes paid tribute to the power of volcanoes by making sacrificial offerings to them. Literature abounds with stories of the volcanoes' staggering power, and, since major active volcanoes are located on every continent, there are obvious ties to social studies.

The third set of activities related to natural disasters examines the mathematics of hurricanes. The word *hurricane* is derived from the name of the

West Indian god of storms, Huracan. These tropical storms have local names, depending on where they originate. In the Pacific, they are called typhoons; in the Atlantic, hurricanes; in the Indian Ocean, cyclones; and in Australia, willy willies. Meteorology is a significant part of the middle school science curriculum. By studying the anatomy of hurricanes and typhoons, following the development of tropical storms, and keeping a "hurricane watch," students find the study of weather a fascinating topic in their science and social studies classes. In the mathematics class, students learn to appreciate the power of tropical storms by working through mathematical activities.

And finally, what student hasn't heard of Dorothy's trip from Kansas to the Land of Oz on the winds of a tornado? Mathematics and science lessons begin in the literature class! Tornadoes are one of nature's most amazing and frightening storms. They reach down out of thunderclouds with wind speeds that range from 200 to 300 miles per hour. If a tornado touches ground, the damage to life and property can be enormous.

In some of the activities in this book, both standard U.S. and metric measurements have been included. Either may be used in the solution of the problems.

EARTHQUAKES

Teacher's Planning Information

Background Information and Procedures

Explain to students that earthquakes are caused by a sudden movement of the Earth. For hundreds of millions of years, the forces of plate tectonics have shaped the Earth. Huge plates that form the surface of the Earth move slowly over, under, and past each other. These are solid and resist the motion of neighboring plates. When one plate gives way to the motion of a neighbor, the result is a powerful release of energy—resulting in earthquake waves. Additional information about earthquakes can be found at the end of the chapter where Additional Readings and informative Internet Web sites are described.

Just how powerful is powerful? The severity of earthquakes can be expressed in several ways—in terms of magnitude or intensity. The *magnitude* of an earthquake, usually expressed by the Richter scale, is a measure of the amplitude of the seismic waves as recorded on a seismograph. We can think of this as indicating the strength or energy released by the earthquake. The *intensity* is measured by criteria that can be seen on the Modified Mercalli Intensity Scale. This is a subjective measure that describes how strong a shock was felt at a particular location and describes the level of damage. The table below shows both of these scales and their measures of magnitude or intensity.

The activity "Significant Earthquakes Around the World—2005" asks students to organize and analyze a large quantity of data on a frequency table and draw a pie graph to visually represent the data. (Up-to-date information can be obtained at http://neic.usgs.gov/neis/ for the years following 2005.) Students can check back at this Web site to get more up-to-date information.

Earthquakes give mathematics teachers a real-world application for logarithmic numbers—a seldom-used mathematical notation skill. These are actually powers of 10. For example, $10^2 = 100$; the log of 100 = 2. If students have a scientific calculator, it should contain a key that changes 10^x to logarithmic numbers and vice versa. Read and discuss the

Mathematical Connections:
Exponential notation, organizing and analyzing data, rational numbers, volume, and graphic representation

Other Curricular Connections:
Earth science, plate tectonics, social studies, journal writing

Concepts:
Students will:

- Examine significant earthquakes and make a pie graph of the data
- Compute the difference in magnitude of exponential numbers
- Subtract decimals
- Use scientific calculators to compute differences in magnitude
- Work collaboratively to problem-solve volume of a rectangular prism

Materials Needed:
- Scientific calculators (10^x or y^x key is needed)
- Copies of all earthquake student worksheets
- Protractors, rulers, and colored pencils (or markers)

example on the "Magnitude of Earthquakes" student worksheet with the students. To compute the difference in magnitude, students must find the difference between the exponents. For example, an earthquake with a magnitude of 5 could be written as 10^5. An earthquake with a magnitude of 7 could be written as 10^7. The difference is 10^2, or 100 times the magnitude. Students will need to use calculators to compute the difference in magnitude when the exponents are decimal fractions.

The next lesson asks students, "How Deep Is Deep?" Working in groups of five or six, students are asked to estimate the number of people that might fit in a hole that is 3 feet (1 m) wide and 40 feet (12 m) deep. For the purposes of this problem, it is assumed that the hole formed was, in fact, a rectangular prism. It is important that students understand that the irregular shape has been modified for the purposes of this problem.

Assessment

1. Student products—Accuracy of worksheets provided in the activities

2. Journal question: "Explain the difference in magnitude between an earthquake in China registering 8.5 on the Richter scale and one in California registering 6.6." [Ans.: $\approx$ 794 times more powerful]

Earthquakes—Selected Answers

Significant Earthquakes Around the World—2005, rounded to the nearest percent and nearest degree:

Answers to "Significant Earthquakes Around the World—2005" Activities

Magnitude	Fraction	Percent	Degrees
8.0–8.9	1/63	2%	7°
7.0–7.9	7/63	11%	40°
6.0–6.9	33/63	52%	187°
5.0–5.9	12/63	19%	68°
4.0–4.9	10/63	16%	58°
TOTAL	**63/63**	**100%**	**360°**

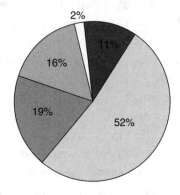

Magnitude of Earthquakes: (1) 10; (2) $\approx$ 3 times more powerful; (3) Many factors can affect the destructive force of earthquakes including building structures, soil, etc. A good site where students can go for hands-on experiences is http://tlc.discovery.com/convergence/quakes/interactives/makeaquake.html

How Deep Is Deep?: (1) The volume of the prism is $3 \times 3 \times 40$ or 360 ft^3; (2) The number of students is an open-ended problem with more than one possible answer.

Comparison of the Modified Mercalli Scale and the Richter Scale

Modified Mercalli Scale	Intensity	Level of Damage	Magnitude (as a power of 10)	Richter Scale
1–4	Instrumental to Moderate	No damage. Very weak.	10^0–10^3	≤ 4.3
5	Rather Strong	Damage negligible. Small, unstable objects displaced. Some dishes or glasses may be broken.	10^3	4.4–4.8
6	Strong	Damage slight. Windows, dishes, glassware broken. Furniture may be moved or overturned. Weak plaster and masonry may crack.	10^3–10^4	4.9–5.4
7	Very Strong	Damage moderate in well-built structure but considerable in poorly built structures. Furniture and weak chimneys broken. Loose bricks, tiles, plaster, and stones may fall.	10^4–10^5	5.5–6.1
8	Destructive	Damage to structures considerable, particularly if they are poorly built. Chimneys, elevated water tanks may fail. Frame houses may move and trees are damaged. Cracks appear in wet ground and steep slopes.	10^5	6.2–6.5
9	Ruinous	Structural damage severe; some buildings will collapse. Serious damage to reservoirs and underground pipes, Conspicuous cracks in ground.	10^5	6.6–6.9
10	Disastrous	Most masonry and frame structures/ foundations destroyed. Some well-built wooden structures and bridges destroyed. Serious damage to dams, dikes, and embankments. Sand and mud shifting on beaches and flat land.	10^6	7.0–7.3
11	Very Disastrous	Few or no masonry structures remain standing. Bridges destroyed. Broad fissures in ground. Underground pipelines completely out of service. Rails bent. Widespread landslides.	10^6–10^7	7.4–8.1
12	Catastrophic	Damage nearly total. Large rock masses displaced. Lines of sight and level distorted. Great devastation and loss of life.	10^7–10^8	> 8.1

Source: Adapted from various sites including http://fema.gov

Significant Earthquakes Around the World—2005

Name _____

Date _____ Class _____

It is estimated that although there are 500,000 detectable earthquakes in the world each year, only 100,000 of those can be felt, and 100 of them cause damage. Let's examine this list of 2005's significant earthquakes (from January 1 to September 9).

Date	Magnitude	Date	Magnitude	Date	Magnitude	Date	Magnitude
Jan. 1	6.6	Feb. 16	6.6	Apr. 11	6.7	June 15	6.5
Jan. 10	5.4	Feb. 19	6.5	Apr. 11	6.8	June 16	4.9
Jan. 10	5.4	Feb. 22	6.5	Apr. 19	5.5	June 17	6.7
Jan. 12	6.8	Feb. 26	6.8	May 1	4.5	June 20	4.7
Jan. 16	6.6	Mar. 2	7.1	May 3	4.9	July 2	6.6
Jan. 19	6.5	Mar. 2	4.9	May 5	6.5	July 5	6.7
Jan. 23	6.2	Mar. 5	5.8	May 12	6.5	July 23	6.0
Jan. 25	4.8	Mar. 9	5.0	May 14	6.8	July 24	7.3
Jan. 25	5.9	Mar. 12	5.7	May 16	6.6	July 25	5.0
Feb. 2	4.8	Mar. 14	5.8	May 19	6.9	Aug. 5	5.2
Feb. 5	6.6	Mar. 14	4.9	May 23	4.3	Aug. 13	4.8
Feb. 5	7.1	Mar. 20	6.6	June 4	6.1	Aug. 16	7.2
Feb. 8	6.8	Mar. 21	6.9	June 6	5.7	Aug. 21	5.1
Feb. 14	6.1	Mar. 28	8.7	June 13	7.8	Sept. 9	7.7
Feb. 15	6.1	Apr. 10	6.7	June 14	6.8		
Feb. 15	5.5	Apr. 10	6.5	June 15	7.2		

Source: http://neic.usgs.gov/neis/eqlists/sig_2005.html

Directions: Working with a partner, use the significant earthquake data to complete the table below. Use your analysis of the data to answer the questions that follow.

Frequency Table

Magnitude	Tally	Fraction	Percent	How Many Degrees of a Circle?
8.0–8.9				
7.0–7.9				
6.0–6.9				
5.0–5.9				
4.0–4.9				
TOTAL				

1. Do you think the data shown represent all of the earthquakes that occurred in 2005? Why or why not?

2. Based on your analysis of the data and the information provided, predict how many earthquakes greater than 7.0 will occur, on average, in any given year. Explain your reasoning.

Significant Earthquakes Around the World—2005

Name _____

Title of graph _____

Make a circle graph that represents the data on the Frequency Table.

Circle Graph

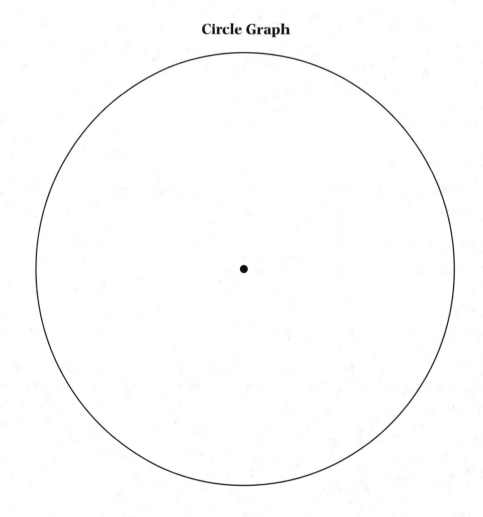

Magnitude of Earthquakes

Name _____

Date _____ Class _____

The difference in magnitude of earthquakes can be expressed as exponents with a base of 10. For example: There are two earthquakes, one with a magnitude of 5 and the other 7; the difference is 2. This means that one of these earthquakes is 10^2, or 100 times as powerful as the other. On the table below are 10 of the most powerful earthquakes of the twentieth century. The difference between 9.5 and 9.2 is 0.3. Using a calculator, we find that $10^{0.3} = 2$. This means that an earthquake registering 9.5 is twice as powerful as one that registers 9.2. Use your calculators to answer the questions below.

Ten Most Powerful Earthquakes		
Year	Location	Richter Scale
1960	Chile	9.5
1964	Prince William Sound, Alaska	9.2
2004	Off the Coast of Northern Sumatra	9.0
1952	Kamchatka, Russia	9.0
1906	Off the Coast of Ecuador	8.8
2005	Northern Sumatra, Indonesia	8.7
1965	Rat Island, Alaska	8.6
1957	Andreanof Islands, Alaska	8.6
1950	Assam, Tibet	8.6
1963	Kuril Islands, Northern Pacific Ocean	8.5

Source: http://neic.usgs.gov

1. How much more powerful is an earthquake that registers 9.5 than one that registers 8.5?

2. How much more powerful was the earthquake off the coast of Chile than the one in Kamchatka?

3. In 1976, an earthquake in Tangshan, China, registered 7.9 on the Richter scale. The death toll has been estimated at about 250,000 people. Yet only 125 people died because of the earthquake (and resulting tsunami) in Prince William Sound, although it registered 9.2 on the Richter scale. Do some research and determine why sometimes there is greater loss of life in earthquakes with lower magnitudes.

How Deep Is Deep?

Name _____

Date _____ Class _____

The 1964 earthquake that occurred in Prince William Sound, Alaska, lasted for 7 minutes. During this earthquake, the ground rolled like waves on the ocean and huge cracks opened in the ground. How deep were these cracks? Some were 3 feet wide and 40 feet deep! Many buildings fell into these deep crevices.

If the crack in the Earth were a square prism with sides of 3 feet and a depth of 40 feet, what would be the volume of this hole? How many students would fit in a hole this size? Work with your classmates to find a solution to this problem. Write your solution in the space provided.

The approximate number of students who would fit in the hole: _____

The volume of the hole: _____

How we solved these problems:

VOLCANOES

Teacher's Planning Information

Background Information and Procedures

Mathematical Connections:
Data collection, ratio and proportion, scale drawing, computation, measurement

Other Curricular Connections:
Meteorology, Earth science, environmental geology, geography, myths and legends, journal writing

Concepts:
Students will:

- Develop a conceptual understanding of the magnitude of the force of volcanoes through mathematical activities
- Use measurements of length to compute distance and rate
- Use ratio and proportion to design a scale drawing of the world's volcanoes
- Work collaboratively to problem-solve rate problems

Materials Needed:
- Rulers and yardsticks
- Maps
- Calculators
- Copies of all volcano student worksheets
- Colored pencils or markers

Ask students how they would define a volcano. If they need some background information, a volcano is a mountain that opens downward into a pool of molten rock below the surface of the earth. When pressure builds up, eruptions may occur causing lava flows, hot ash flows, mudslides, avalanches, tsunamis, and earthquakes. Volcanoes have awesome power! When Mount St. Helens erupted in Washington State, a piece of rock the size of the Empire State Building was blown off the top. It had been dormant for over 100 years and when it erupted it took the lives of 58 people and caused more than $1.2 billion in damage. There are more than 500 active volcanoes in the world; more than half of these are part of the "Ring of Fire" that encircles the Pacific Ocean. Most of the volcanoes in the United States are found in Hawaii, Alaska, California, Oregon, and Washington.

The Volcanic Explosivity Index (VEI) is used to measure the magnitude of volcanic eruptions—it is based upon the height of the plume and the volume of the eruption.

The mathematics lessons in this unit are divided into two parts. For the first lesson, "Some Interesting Facts About Volcanoes," students work in groups of four to solve the problems. The first problem is open-ended; it is possible for different groups to get different answers. It is important to discuss the strategies that each group used, as well as their solution. The other problems can be solved using ratio/proportion or the formula $D = r \cdot t$. The answers should be a consensus of the group—the results should come from group discussion and collaboration.

The Volcanic Explosivity Index

VEI (Category)	Description	Plume Height	Volume
0	Non-explosive	< 100 m	1,000 m^3
1	Gentle	100–1000 m	10,000 m^3
2	Explosive	1–5 km	1,000,000 m^3
3	Severe	3–15 km	10,000,000 m^3
4	Cataclysmic	10–25 km	100,000,000 m^3
5	Paroxysmal	> 25 km	1 km^3
6	Colossal	> 25 km	10 km^3
7	No Description	> 25 km	100 km^3
8	No Description	> 25 km	1,000 km^3

Source: http://www.fema.gov/kids/intense.htm#volcanic

The second lesson has students use a table of volcanoes, with one volcano representing each continent. Working alone, each student designs a "graph" of volcanoes using an appropriate scale. These drawings can be enhanced by using colored pencils or markers.

Some of the activities express the data using both standard U.S. and metric units of measure.

Assessment

1. Student products—Successful completion of student worksheets

2. Journal question: "When Mount Tolbachik erupted in 1975, the lava gushed out at a speed of 550 feet per second. Express this speed in miles per hour."

   [Ans.: 550 ft./sec. = 3300 ft./1 min(60sec) = 198,000 ft./1 hr.; 198,000 ft. ÷ 5,280 ft. = 37.5 mi. The lava flowed at a rate of 37.5 mi./hr.]

Volcanoes—Selected Answers:

Some Interesting Facts About Volcanoes: (1) Answers will vary; (2) 600 seconds or 10 minutes; (3) ≈ 45.5 atmospheres of pressure; ≈ 683.5 lb./sq. in. [(45.5 × 14.7) + 14.7 for the surface]

Volcanic Mountains Grid: Scales used may vary.

Some Interesting Facts About Volcanoes

Name _____

Date _____ Class _____

1. Some lava flows can be 66 feet (about 20 meters) thick and take several years to cool. Work with your group to determine how many students, standing side by side, it would take to form a line 66 feet (20 meters) long.

   We decided it would take _____ students to form a line 66 feet (20 meters) long.

   How we solved this problem: _____

   _____

2. The loudest sound ever recorded occurred in 1883. It was the eruption of a volcano on the island of Krakatau in the Pacific Ocean. The noise was heard as far away as Australia (about 3,000 miles away).

   If sound travels at a speed of about 1 mile every 5 seconds, how long did it take for the sound to travel from Krakatau to Australia? (Be sure to use appropriate units of measure.)

   We decided it would take _____ for sound to travel from Krakatau to Australia.

   How we solved this problem: _____

3. Crater Lake in Oregon was formed by a powerful volcanic eruption about 6,600 years ago. It is the deepest lake in the United States, with an average depth of 1,500 feet.

   Pressure increases the deeper you go down in water. Pressure increases at a rate of approximately 1 atmosphere of pressure for every 33 feet. One atmosphere of pressure is approximately 14.7 pounds per square inch. If 1 atmosphere is added to the pressure that occurs at the surface:

   There would be _____ atmospheres of pressure at a depth of 1,500 feet.

   The pressure on each square inch of an object would be _____.

   How we solved this problem: _____

Volcanic Mountains Grid

Name _____

Date _____ Class _____

There are more than 600 active volcanoes on Earth. About half of these are located in the Ring of Fire. This ring encircles the Pacific Ocean, both on land and underwater. Volcanoes are found on every continent:

Continent	Country	Volcano	Height
Africa	Zaire	Nyirangongo	11,546 ft.
Antarctica	Ross Island	Erebus	12,202 ft.
Asia	Russia	Kluchevskaya	15,580 ft.
Europe	Italy	Mt. Etna	10,955 ft.
North America	United States	Mt. St. Helens	14,006 ft.
South America	Argentina	Antofalla	20,097 ft.
Oceania	New Zealand	Ruapehu	9,174 ft.

Use the graph on the next page to draw a two-dimensional sketch of each of these volcanic mountains to scale. (The information you will need for your scale drawing can be found above.) Each square on the grid is 1/4 inch. You will have to work out a scale so that the tallest of the mountains will fit on the page.

The scale I used: _____

The reason I used this scale: _____

_____

Volcanic Mountains Grid

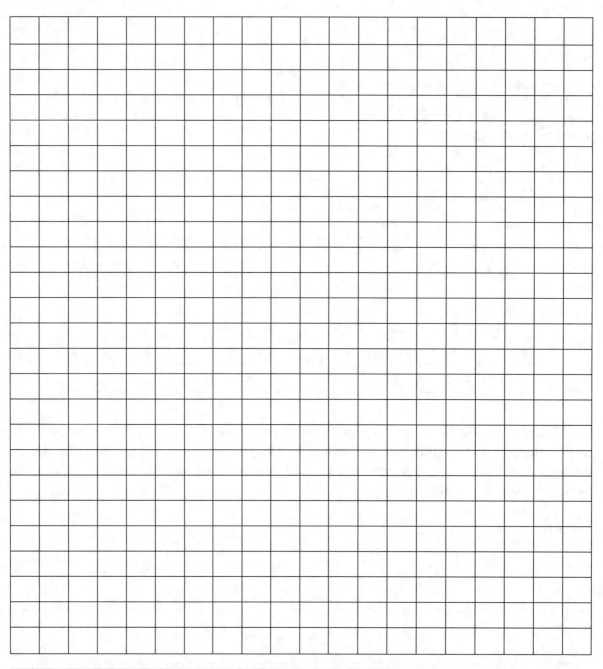

HURRICANES

Teacher's Planning Information

Background Information and Procedures

During the summer and fall of 2005, the Gulf Coast and the eastern part of the United States were hit with some devastating hurricanes, including Katrina and Rita. A hurricane is a tropical storm with winds that have reached a constant speed of 74 miles per hour or more. The Saffir-Simpson Hurricane Scale—with a 1 to 5 rating—is used to estimate the speed of the winds, the potential damage, and the flooding expected along the coast from the hurricane's landfall. The following table of the Saffir-Simpson scale may be copied and used as part of the class discussion on the power and magnitude of hurricanes.

Hurricanes need warm tropical oceans, moisture, and light winds above them. If the right conditions last long enough, a hurricane can produce violent winds, incredible waves, torrential rains, and floods. While the hurricane season officially begins in the United States on June 1 and ends November 30, the majority of hurricanes occur in August and September because the oceans have warmed sufficiently to provide the necessary conditions. The activity "Frequency of U.S. Hurricanes" asks students to analyze the data of hurricane frequency by month from 1851 to 2004. They are then asked to design a graph to represent the data.

Hurricane damage results from storm surge, wind, and inland flooding from heavy rainfall. While water rarely falls uniformly in a large area, the activity "How Much Water?" makes the assumption that water from the storm is at a uniform depth and asks students, "How much water actually falls when 1 inch of rain uniformly falls on an area? How much does it weigh? What is its volume?" The answers to these questions are incredible!

Mathematical Connections:
Standard U.S. measurement conversions, computation, estimation, percentages, graphic representation

Other Curricular Connections:
Meteorology, Earth science, environmental geology, geography, history, literature, journal writing

Concepts:
Students will:

- Calculate percentages
- Draw a graph to represent a set of data
- Use standard U.S. measurements to find the volume of large quantities of water
- Use standard U.S. measurements to find the weight of large quantities of water
- Estimate the relative size of large quantities of water

Materials Needed:
- calculators
- world almanacs or world atlases
- student worksheets for each group of students

Saffir-Simpson Hurricane Scale			
Category	Wind Speed	Storm Surge	Level of Damage
1	74–95 mi/hr. (119–153 km/hr.)	4–5 ft. (1.2–1.5 m)	Primary damage is to mobile homes and trees. There might be some coastal flooding but there is little damage to permanent building structures. Ex.: Hurricane Gaston—2004
2	96–110 mi/hr. (154–177 km/hr.)	6–8 ft. (1.8–2.4 m)	Considerable damage to mobile homes and trees. Some trees may be blown down. Buildings sustain roof and window damage. Ex: Hurricane Frances—2004
3	111–130 mi/hr. (178–209 km/hr.)	9–12 ft. (2.7–3.4 m)	Mobile homes destroyed. Some structural damage to small homes. Large trees may be blown down. There is flooding near the coastline, and areas that are lower than 5 ft. (1.5 m) above mean sea level may be flooded up to 8 miles (13 km) inland or more. Evacuation within blocks of the shoreline may be required. Ex: Hurricanes Jeanne and Ivan—2004
4	131–155 mi/hr. (210–249 km/hr.)	13–18 ft. (4.0–5.5 m)	Complete destruction of mobile homes, and roofs destroyed on homes. Extensive damage to beaches and boats. Escape routes may be cut off by rising water. Areas lower than 10 ft. (3 m) may be flooded as far inland as 6 miles (10 km) requiring massive evacuation. Ex: Hurricane Charley—2004, and Hurricane Katrina—2005
5	> 155 mi/hr. (> 249 km/hr.)	> 18 ft. (> 5.5 m)	Complete roof failure of most homes and buildings with trees uprooted or blown down. If the area is less than 15 ft. (4.6 m) above sea level, there is major flooding of the lower floors of all structures within 500 yards of the shoreline. Massive evacuation of residential areas on low ground within 5 to 10 miles (8–16 km) of shoreline may be required. Only three Category 5 hurricanes have made landfall in the United States since official records began: The Labor Day Hurricane—1935, Hurricane Camille—1969, and Hurricane Andrew—1992

Source: http://www.nhc.noaa.gov/aboutsshs.shtml

Use the information on the "How Much Water?" (p. 24) student worksheet to help students calculate and understand how much 1 inch of water would weigh if the floor of their classroom were covered with rain. While this is not likely to happen, an area that is visible to students is more understandable. Let's assume your classroom is 30 ft. × 30 ft. One square mile contains 27,878,400 square feet. A classroom with the dimensions above is 900 square feet. One inch of water over 1 square mile of land equals 17,371,520 gallons. Using the decimal ratio for

$$\frac{900}{27,878,400}$$

we find that the classroom would have about 521 gallons of water on the floor (0.00003 × 17,371,520). This much water would weigh about 4,324.3 pounds! Students can actually measure the area of the classroom floor and calculate the volume and weight of 1 inch of water for their own classroom.

Hurricane Katrina (in September 2005), a Category 4 hurricane, caused tremendous damage in New Orleans because the winds and the water surge destroyed parts of the levee system. When over 20 feet of water flooded the city, the damage was unbelievable. Students can use maps or Internet information to find the area of New Orleans that was underwater and calculate the weight and volume of that devastating flood.

Assessment:

1. Student products—Accuracy of worksheet

2. Journal question: "If you had a 50-gallon fish tank in your bedroom, how much would the water inside it weigh? What information would you need to compute the weight exerted on each square foot of floor space?" [Ans.: 50 gal. × 8.3 lb. = 415 lb. You would need to know the dimensions of the tank.]

Hurricanes—Selected Answers:

Frequency of U.S. Hurricanes: (1) ≈ 37%; (2) Tropical storms need warm water to grow into the intensity of hurricanes. A good site for students to explore to get more information on "what makes a hurricane" is http://kids.earth.nasa.gov/archive/hurricane/

How Much Water? (1) ≈ 1.8×10^{12} gallons of water fell—(3,459 × 30 × 17,371,520); the water weighed ≈ 1.5×10^{13} lb.—(1.8×10^{12} × 8.3) (2) ≈ 1.05×10^{14} gallons of water fell—(261,914 × 30 × 17,371,520); the water weighed ≈ 8.7×10^{14}—(1.05×10^{14} × 8.3) (3) Answers will vary—bathtub capacity can vary from 45 gallons to over 60 gallons depending on the tub's features. Swimming pools have a much greater variation. The formula to use to find the capacity of a pool (in gallons) is: Length × Width × Average depth of water × 7.48 (the number of gallons of water per cubic foot). This formula was obtained from http://www.crcwater.org/qwaterequivalents.html. Suppose the students use the following dimensions for their pool: 12′ × 24′ × 42″ (3.5′). Solution: 12 × 24 × 3.5 × 7.48 ≈ 7,540 gal.

Frequency of U.S. Hurricanes

Name _____

Date _____ Class _____

Hurricanes are severe tropical storms that produce violent winds, torrential rains, huge waves, and unbelievable floods. In the United States, hurricanes usually strike the coastal regions between June 1 and November 30. Why do they occur at this time? Hurricanes form over oceans when the water is sufficiently warm at the surface to put enough heat and moisture into the atmosphere to fuel the hurricane. The table below shows the number of hurricane strikes to hit the U.S. mainland from 1851 to 2004.

Directions:

1. Calculate the percentage of the total hurricanes that occurred during each month.

2. Then, work with your partner to compute the answers to the questions on the next page.

Hurricane Strikes to Hit the U.S. Mainland From 1851–2004

Month	Hurricanes in the U.S.	Percentage
June	19	
July	23	
August	74	
September	102	
October	50	
November	5	
TOTAL	**273**	

Source: http://www.nhc.noaa.gov

1. What percentage of the hurricanes occurred in September? _____

2. Most of the hurricanes occurred in the months of August, September, and October. Why do you think this is the case?

3. Activity: Design a graph to illustrate the data shown on the table.

How Much Water?

Name _____

Date _____ Class _____

The most violent and powerful storms are called hurricanes if they occur over the Atlantic Ocean, typhoons if they occur over the Pacific Ocean, or cyclones if they occur over the Indian Ocean. All of these storms begin over warm waters. The wind speeds of hurricanes can reach more than 200 miles per hour, and their size can measure as much as 500 miles wide. Hurricanes contain enormous quantities of water.

How much water is an enormous amount of water? Let's examine this question. To do so you need to have a little information about the meaning of "1 inch of rain."

> 1 inch of rain on 1 square mile of land $\approx$ 17,371,520 gallons
>
> 1 gallon of water weighs $\approx$ 8.3 pounds

1. Fact: A hurricane that hit Puerto Rico in 1928 dropped 30 inches of rain. (The area of Puerto Rico is 3,459 mi².)

   Question: How many gallons of rain fell on Puerto Rico? _____

   How much did the water weigh that fell on Puerto Rico? _____

2. Fact: In 1921, a hurricane in Texas deposited 23 inches of rain in a single day. (The area of Texas is 261,914 mi².)

   Question: If there was a uniform amount of rain across the state, how many gallons of water fell? _____

   How much did the water weigh? _____

3. Work with your group to estimate just how much water 17,000,000 gallons of water is. How does it compare with the amount of water in a bathtub? In a swimming pool? How did you solve this problem?

TORNADOES

Teacher's Planning Information

Background Information and Procedures

Tornadoes are one of nature's most violent storms. Approximately 1,000 tornadoes are reported across the United States each year. A tornado is a violently rotating column of air and is capable of tremendous destruction with wind speeds of 250 miles per hour or more. Damage paths can be in excess of 1 mile wide and 50 miles long.

What is a tornado? The whirlpool that forms in a bathtub, sink, or toilet when the water is draining is essentially an example of the science behind tornadoes. A vortex is exemplified by the "spinning skater effect." As a spinning skater draws up her arms (and forms the shape of a tornado), she spins more rapidly. The winds of tornadoes are the fastest on Earth. And unlike the events in *The Wizard of Oz*, real tornadoes roar like freight trains, whip out of clouds, and when they reach the earth's surface, cause destruction of enormous proportions. Over water, the spinning storms create giant water spouts. In deserts, the spinning air columns produce dust devils, and over land, the columns act as giant vacuum cleaners, sucking up everything in their paths.

Tornadoes are measured using the Fujita Tornado Damage Scale (also called the Fujita scale or F-scale). This can be copied and discussed with students.

Mathematical Connections:
Measurement, computation, estimation, using formulas, conversions

Other Curricular Connections:
Meteorology. Earth science, geography, history, current events, journal writing, literature

Concepts:
Students will:

- Calculate time when the rate and distance are known
- Estimate distance
- Predict distance of lightning strikes based on time differential

Materials Needed:
- Calculators
- Yardsticks and tape measures
- Copies of student tornado worksheets

Some tornadoes may form during the early stages of rapidly developing thunderstorms. This type of tornado is most common along the front range of the Rocky Mountains, the Plains, and the Western states. Because some thunderstorms are accompanied by severe lightning, the first lesson introduces students to the relationship between lightning and thunder. Students are asked to count the number of seconds between seeing lightning and hearing thunder. They actually occur at the same time, but since sound travels much slower than

Fujita Tornado Damage Scale

Category	Wind Speed in mph	Observable Damage
F-0	40–72	Light damage: Some damage to chimneys; branches broken off trees; shallow-rooted trees pushed over; signboards damaged.
F-1	73–112	Moderate damage: Peels surface off roofs; mobile homes pushed off foundations or overturned; moving cars blown off roads.
F-2	113–157	Considerable damage: Roofs torn off frame houses; mobile homes demolished; railroad cars overturned; large trees severely damaged or uprooted; cars lifted off ground.
F-3	158–206	Severe damage: Roofs and some walls torn off well-constructed houses, trains overturned, most trees in forest uprooted; heavy cars lifted off ground and thrown.
F-4	207–260	Devastating damage: Well-constructed houses leveled; structures with weak foundations blown off some distance; cars thrown and large missiles produced.
F-5	261–318	Incredible damage: Strong frame houses lifted off foundations and swept away; automobile-sized missiles fly through the air in excess of 100 meters (328 feet); trees debarked; incredible phenomena will occur.

Source: http://www.spc.noaa.gov/faq/tornado/f-scale.html

light, we see the lightning before we hear the thunder. The data below give some interesting mathematical relationships between the speeds of lightning and thunder (light and sound).

> The speed of light (in a vacuum) $\approx$ 186,000 mi/sec.
>
> The speed of sound (in air) $\approx$ 760 mph or 0.21 mi/sec.

The first activity relates to the relative speeds of light and sound and the connection between rapidly developing thunderstorms and tornadoes. The second activity deals with some interesting phenomena related to tornadoes and asks students to perform some calculations to better understand what happened.

Discuss with students their impression of tornadoes based on their knowledge of *The Wizard of Oz*. A video showing the tornado scenes depicted in the movie might be shown. Interactive Web sites, discussed at the end of this chapter, give students the opportunity to see tornadoes and their impact.

Assessment:

1. Successful completion of activity sheets

2. Journal question: "Explain why we see lightning strike sooner than we hear the accompanying thunder." [Ans.: Because the speed of light is over 885,000 times faster than the speed of sound.]

Tornadoes—Selected Answers:

The Science of Lightning: (1) 0.21 mi/sec. (760 ÷ 3,600); (2) ≈ 0.84 mile away; (3) ≈ 6.3 miles away; answers will vary.

Some Interesting Facts About Tornadoes: (1) Answers will vary; (2) 4 hours, 30 minutes; (3) Answers will vary.

The Science of Lightning

Name _____

Date _____ Class _____

During every minute of every day, roughly 2,000 thunderstorms creating lightning occur somewhere on Earth. Though the chances of being struck by lightning are estimated at 1 in 600,000, these huge electrical sparks are one of the leading causes of weather-related deaths in the USA each year. We can tell how far away lightning is when we understand the relationship between the speed of light and the speed of sound.

> Light travels at a rate of 186,000 miles per second (in a vacuum).
>
> Sound travels at a rate of 760 miles per hour (in air).

Use this information and work with your partner to solve these problems:

1. What is the rate of sound expressed in mi/sec.?

   How we solved this problem:

2. You see a flash of lightening and 4 seconds later you hear the thunder. About how far away did the lightening strike?

   How we solved this problem:

3. The Illinois High School Association (IHSA) has a 30–30 rule that applies to sporting events and other outdoor activities: "A combination of the 30 second flash-to-bang count to suspend play and the 30-minute delay after the last lightning flash to resume activity." (http://www.ihsa.org/org/lightning.htm)

   How far away is the lightning strike if there are 30 seconds from "flash to bang"?

   Why do you think they require a 30-minute delay after the last lightning strike?

Some Interesting Facts About Tornadoes

Name _____

Date _____ Class _____

Tornadoes are funnel-shaped storms that twist as air spins upward. This whirling motion, called a vortex, is an efficient method to shift liquids and gases quickly. An example of how the vortex works is the "spinning skater effect." As a skater draw her arms upward, she turns more rapidly. In the center of tornadoes, winds can reach speeds of more than 250 miles per hour.

These powerful storms or *twisters* have given us some interesting tales.

1. The Super Outbreak of April 3 to 4, 1974, lasted 16 hours and produced a total of 148 tornadoes. It went across 13 states: Alabama, Georgia, Illinois, Indiana, Kentucky, Michigan, Mississippi, North Carolina, Ohio, South Carolina, Tennessee, Virginia, and West Virginia. It covered a path of over 2,500 miles. Work with your group to find what lies within a circle around your town that has a diameter of 2,500 miles.

   We found the following:

2. On May 26, 1917, a single tornado traveled at an average speed of 65 miles per hour for 293 miles.

   The tornado traveled for _____ hours and _____ minutes.

   How we solved this problem:

3. On September 4, 1981, a tornado hit Ancona, Italy. It lifted a sleeping baby in its crib 50 feet in the air and carried it 328 feet away. The baby slept through the whole trip and was set down safely. If you traveled 328 feet from your classroom, where in the school would you be?

ADDITIONAL READING

Adoff, A. (1977). *Tornado! Poems.* New York: Delacarta Press.

A poetic description of a tornado and its aftermath.

Billout, G. (1981). *Thunderbolt and rainbow: A look at Greek mythology.* Englewood Cliffs, NJ: Prentice Hall.

This book examines the many myths and legends surrounding natural phenomena such as hurricanes, volcanoes, and so forth.

Cottonwood, J. (1995). *Quake.* New York: Scholastic.

Fourteen-year-old Franny is alone with her younger brother and cousin in her home on Loma Prieta Mountain, California, when an earthquake destroys it. This story tells how they cope with fear and danger.

DeSpain, P. (1994). *Eleven turtle tales: Adventure tales from around the world.* Little Rock, AR: August House.

A collection of folk tales from around the world. One of them, a Native American tale, tells the story of how the Great Spirit formed California on the back of giant turtles and why there are earthquakes.

Eubank, M. (2004). *Weather detectives.* Lawton, UT: Gibbs Smith.

Two young weather detectives escape dust storm on Mars, learn about cloudbursts and hurricanes in Florida, and find out about freezing rain in Alabama. They experience the highest and lowest recorded temperatures, huge hailstones, and snowflakes as large as pizzas.

George, J. C. (1966). *One day in the prairie.* New York: Crowell.

A nonfiction account of how the animals on a prairie wildlife preserve sense an approaching tornado and attempt to protect themselves before it touches down.

Kudlinski, K. V. (1993). *Earthquake: A story of old San Francisco.* New York: Viking.

In 1906, after the infamous San Francisco earthquake, 12-year-old Phillip struggles to save the horses in his family's livery stable.

Lowell, S. (1993). *I Am Lavina Cumming.* Minneapolis, MN: Milkweed.

The death of 10-year-old Lavina's mother makes it necessary for her to stay with relatives in San Francisco. Her adventures include living through the great earthquake of 1906.

O'Meara, D. (2005). *Into the volcano: A volcano researcher at work.* Tonawanda, NY: Kids Can Press.

Photographer Donna O'Meara and her husband share their thrilling experiences that take them from Kilauea (Hawaii) to Stomboli (Italy). Each experience illustrates a different type of volcano and looks at the culture of the people affected by these forces of nature.

Sakany, L., & Asher, D. (2003). *Hurricane hunters and tornado chasers: Life in the eye of the storm.* New York: Rosen.

Describes the destructive forces behind severe weather systems such as tornadoes and hurricanes and the experiences of people interested in researching and tracking these storms.

Simon, S. (1981). *Einstein Anderson makes up for lost time.* New York: Viking.

Einstein Anderson, a science sleuth, uses his scientific knowledge to solve a variety of puzzles, including inventing a machine that can stop hurricanes.

Thompson, L. (2000). *Tsunamis.* New York: Children's Press.

This book recaps the tsunami caused by an earthquake on Mindoro Island in the Philippines in 1994 and discusses how tsunamis start and how they move. Readers will be fascinated to learn that a tsunami can pass beneath a ship and not be felt, but it is a very different story as it approaches land.

Vogel, C. G. (2001). *Native American lore and the science of weather.* Brookfield, CT: Millbrook Press.

This book presents weather from the standpoint of Native American storytellers who recount legends related to the sun, wind, and clouds.

Winthrop, E. (1984). *Belinda's hurricane.* New York: Dutton.

This book tells the adventures of Belinda and her grandmother as they wait out a hurricane on Fox Island.

Wyatt, V. (2000). *Weather: Frequently asked questions.* Toronto, ON, Canada: Kids Can Press.

How can a tornado pluck the feathers off a chicken? How can you make lightning in your mouth? Have you ever wondered how big a raindrop is? This book will teach you about all of these topics and will illustrate some fun and educational experiments as well.

INTERNET WEB SITES

Weather

http://www.noaa.gov

The Web site for the National Oceanic and Atmospheric Administration. It contains up-to-date information about a variety of weather-related phenomena and natural disasters including droughts, floods, hurricanes, lightning, tornadoes, tsunamis, and volcanoes, as well as air quality and past and present weather information.

Earthquakes

http://neic.usgs.gov

The Web site of the National Earthquake Information Center (NEIC). The NEIC determines the location and size of all destructive earthquakes worldwide and immediately disseminates this information to concerned national and international agencies, scientists, and the general public via this Web site.

http://earthquake.usgs.gov/recenteqs

An interactive site that allows students to view earthquakes that occurred in the United States almost up to the minute—from one hour ago to one week ago. By clicking on a particular earthquake site, students learn where it occurred, when it occurred, its magnitude, and more. It is an interesting way for students to learn how many earthquakes actually occur every day, including some we are unaware of because they are not powerful enough to be reported.

http://tlc.discovery.com/convergence/quakes/interactives/makeaquake.html

An interactive section of this Web site, "Make a Quake," gives students the opportunity to choose the type of ground a structure is on, any attempts to fortify the building, and the magnitude of the quake. Then the quake begins and the resultant damage is shown. Site also illustrates the "Top 10 Quakes" with a map showing location, magnitude, the date when each occurred, and casualties. "As the Earth Churns" takes the students from the Archeozoic Era (4.6 billion years ago) to the present with animated drawings.

Volcanoes:

http://www.volcanoes.com

An educational site that has information about volcanoes around the world, how volcanoes work, and links to many other volcano sites.

http://www.learner.org/exhibits/volcanoes

This Web site is a comprehensive educational resource that describes the science behind volcanoes and volcanic processes.

http://volcano.und.edu/volcanoes.html

This Web site keeps up with current eruptions and has information about the Earth's volcanoes by world region, country, and name. It also contains film clips of volcanic eruptions.

Hurricanes:

http://hurricanes.noaa.gov

A governmental agency Web site that contains up-to-date information about current hurricanes and links to historical and scientific information.

http://science.howstuffworks.com/hurricane.htm

A very student-friendly site that defines hurricanes, explains how they form, describes the parts of a hurricane, how hurricanes are tracked, their names, and much more.

http://kids.earth.nasa.gov/archive/hurricane

> One of the NASA Web sites for students, this one has visual and active information about how hurricanes are created, how they move, and how dangerous they are.

Tornadoes:

http://www.noaa.gov/tornadoes.html

> A government site that shows the Fujita Tornado Damage Scale and has many interesting links showing history, location, historical occurrence of tornadoes by states, and most powerful and destructive tornadoes.

http://www.fema.gov/kids/tornado.htm

> Web site of the Federal Emergency Management Agency (FEMA) designed specifically for students. It contains activities and photos, as well as all of the disaster intensity scales.

Physics, Formulas, and Math 2

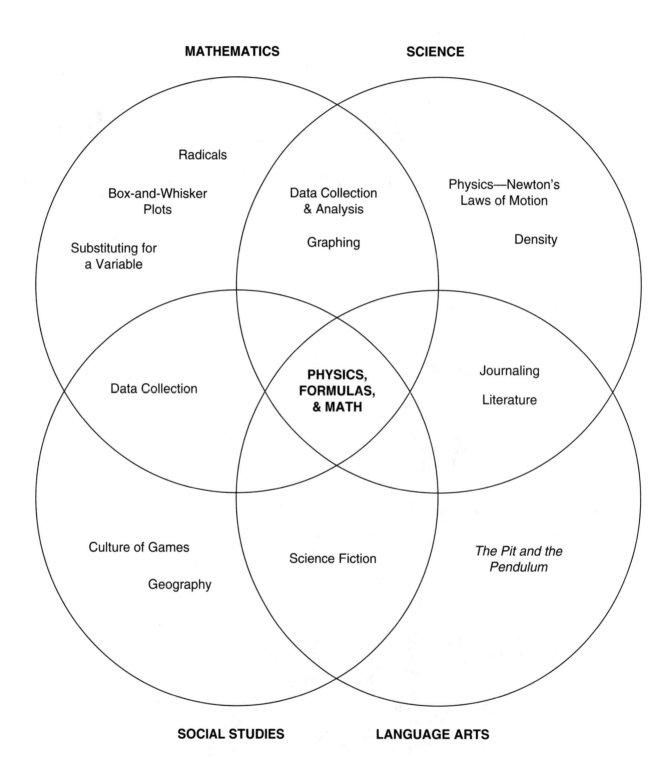

MATHEMATICS   **SCIENCE**

Radicals

Box-and-Whisker
Plots

Data Collection
& Analysis

Physics—Newton's
Laws of Motion

Substituting for
a Variable

Graphing

Density

Data Collection

**PHYSICS,
FORMULAS,
& MATH**

Journaling

Literature

Culture of Games

Geography

Science Fiction

*The Pit and the
Pendulum*

SOCIAL STUDIES   **LANGUAGE ARTS**

Physics, Formulas, and Math

2

No human inquiry can be called science unless it pursues its path through mathematical exposition and demonstration.

—Leonardo da Vinci

INTRODUCTION

Mathematics is used to explain the laws of science. Scientists value mathematics because it is an essential part of the discovery process. In *Science for All Americans: Project 2061* (American Association for the Advancement of Science, 1989), this alliance is described as "having a long history, dating back many centuries. Science provides mathematics with interesting problems to investigate, and mathematics provides science with powerful tools to use in analyzing data" (p. 17).

Mathematics uses abstract symbols as its language. For this reason, the language of mathematics is universal. However, it is also difficult for students to comprehend. Many middle school students are still very concrete in their thinking patterns and are unable to understand the real meaning of abstract formulas such as $V = 4/3\ \pi r^3$ or $d = 1/2\ (9.8\ m^2)$. The activities in this chapter show how mathematics is used to help explain scientific phenomena.

The first activity, "Sports Balls and Density," poses the question, "Will this ball sink or float?" By finding the volume and mass of a variety of sports balls, and calculating the density—by using formulas and variables—students can discover which of the sports balls will sink and which will float.

"Swings of the Pendulum" connects measurement, data collection, Edgar Allan Poe's *The Pit and the Pendulum,* and Newton's laws of motion to get students actively involved in understanding how physical phenomena are explained using mathematics and formulas.

In the activity "Roller Coasters: How Fast Are We Falling?" students discover that although *what goes up must come down,* the rate at which something falls can be found by using the formula for acceleration. Using box-and-whisker plots and coordinate graphs, students experience the power of graphic representation to help us get a "picture the data."

The real-world connection to social studies is a natural: Where in the world are these amusement parks? Can students locate them on a map? Perhaps some of them have visited these parks and could relate their experiences to the class. Books and Web sites can be found at the end of the chapter. Students might enjoy reading them, and language arts teachers might find some motivating stories to use in their classes.

SPORTS BALLS AND DENSITY

Teacher's Planning Information

Background Information and Procedures:

Begin the lesson by holding up a tennis ball and asking students, "Do you think this ball would sink or float in water?" Then hold up a baseball and ask the same question. Students might agree on the tennis ball but there should be some controversy about this last question. Whether an object floats or sinks in water can be determined using a formula.

The density of an object is calculated by this formula:

$$D = \frac{\text{mass}}{\text{volume}}$$

When students are given a sports ball, there are two measurements that must be known—the ball's mass and its volume. The mass is easily obtained: the ball is weighed.

To find the volume of a sphere, students need to know the formula:

$$V = 4/3\pi r^3$$

After students are given this formula, ask them to problem-solve how they might find the radius of a sphere when they cannot measure the line segment that joins the center of this sphere with a point on its surface. In this lesson, students measure the circumference of a sports ball using tape measures or a piece of string and a ruler. Since we know that $C = 2\pi r$ or πd, if students divide the circumference by π, they will have calculated the diameter. Then, by dividing the diameter by 2, they have computed the radius. Once students have found the volume and mass of the sphere, they can substitute these values into the formula and compute the density of the sports balls. All of the linear measurements should be in centimeters and the mass should be measured in grams.

Mathematical Connections:
Geometry and volume, data collection, measurement, algebra concepts

Other Curricular Connections:
Physics, culture of games, language arts

Concepts:
Students will:

- Predict whether each of the sports balls will float or sink when placed in water
- Find the mass and volume of a variety of sports balls
- Use their measurements to calculate the density of each ball using the density formula

Materials Needed:
- A variety of sports balls
- Metric tape measures or string, and metric rulers and scales
- Worksheet of "Finding the Density of a Sports Ball," Pages 1 and 2, for each group of students
- Calculators

For this activity, students will work in groups of four. Assign the following roles:

1. The Measurers: This will require two students—one to hold the tape measure or string and the other to read the measurements as accurately as possible. These students will also be responsible for finding the mass of the sports balls.

2. The Recorder: This student will record the measurements on the "Finding the Density of a Sports Ball—Data Table."

3. The Calculator: This student will use the group's measurements to compute the density of each of the sports balls.

Assessment:

1. Calculations and written responses on students' worksheet, "Finding the Density of a Sports Ball"

2. Journal question: "Explain how you used π to find the density of the sports balls."

Sports Balls and Density—Selected Answers:

Student answers will vary—calculations are based upon their measurements. There should be some leeway given to students' measurements.

Finding the Density of a Sports Ball, Page 1

Name _____

Date _____ Class _____

If the ball you are playing with falls into the water, do you think it will sink or float? Do you think it matters what kind of ball it is? Do you think a soccer ball will float? A baseball? A golf ball? To answer these questions, you need to know the density of the ball. Density is the relationship between the volume and mass of an object. The formula for finding the density of an object is

$$D = \frac{\text{mass}}{\text{volume}}$$

What measurements do we need to take?

1. Find the mass of the ball (we weigh it using a scale).

2. Use the formula to find the volume of the ball (a sphere): $V = 4/3\pi r^3$

3. We measure the circumference of the ball to help us compute the diameter and when we divide that by 2, we have the radius that we need in our formula.

Sound complicated? Well, just take it one step at a time!

1. Divide the circumference of the sphere by π—we now know the diameter of the ball.

2. Divide the diameter in half to get the radius.

Now we have all of the measurements we need to find the density of our sports balls!

Finding the Density of a Sports Ball, Page 2

Enter your measurements on this table and then use them to calculate the density of each of the sports balls.

Finding the Density of a Sports Ball—Data Table

Ball	Mass (in grams)	Circumference (in cm)	Radius $\frac{1}{2}\left(\frac{c}{\pi}\right)$	Volume $\frac{4}{3}\pi r^3$	Density $D = \dfrac{\text{mass}}{\text{volume}}$
Softball					
Soccer Ball					
Volleyball					
Basketball					
Baseball					
Tennis Ball					
Golf Ball					
Ping-Pong Ball					

Which balls have a density > 1? _____

Which balls have a density < 1? _____

Which of these balls do you think will float? Why?

Which do you think will sink? Why?

SWINGS OF THE PENDULUM

Teacher's Planning Information

Background Information and Procedures:

Discuss Poe's story *The Pit and the Pendulum* with students and what might affect the swings of a pendulum. Have students predict whether or not they believe the length of the rope will affect the number of swings per minute or if there are other criteria that might affect the frequency.

What variables might students say will affect a pendulum's swing? They might discuss the following:

1. *Length of the pendulum*—Changing the length of a pendulum while keeping other factors constant changes the length of the period (a period is one swing of the pendulum—back and forth). Longer pendulums swing with a lower frequency than shorter pendulums, and thus have a longer period.

2. *Starting angle of the pendulum*—Changing the starting angle of the pendulum (how far you pull it back to get it started).

3. *Mass of the weight at the end of the pendulum*—Changing the mass of the pendulum bob does not affect the frequency of the pendulum.

4. *Force of gravity*—This accelerates the pendulum's downward swing. The momentum built up by the acceleration of gravity causes the mass to swing in the opposite direction to a height equal to the original position.

This activity can be coordinated with a science teacher as it relates to Newton's laws of motion. There is a formula that can be used to determine the length of time for each period of swing: $P = 1.1\sqrt{l}$ where P = time for each period (back and forth swing) and l = the length of the string. This formula is shown on the "Journal Entry" page where students are asked to

Mathematical Connections:
Measurement data collection and analysis, problem solving

Other Curricular Connections:
Physics, literature

Concepts:
Students will:

- Measure lengths of string in metric units
- Collect and analyze data through experimentation
- Work collaboratively to problem-solve
- Draw conclusions based upon observations
- Make connections between mathematics and physics

Materials Needed:
- Copy of "Swings of the Pendulum" worksheet for each group of students
- Stopwatches or watches (clock) with second hands
- Lengths of string long enough for groups to measure and cut required lengths (25, 50, 100, and 150 cm)
- Washers or other weights (4 for each group)
- Calculators
- Overhead transparency of "Swings of the Pendulum—Class Data Table"

compare their results to the mathematical calculations obtained when using this formula.

Place students into groups of four and assign the following roles in each group:

1. The Recorder: This student records the data for the group.

2. The "Swinger": This student swings the pendulum. By having one student take on this role, the angle of the pendulum will be more consistent with each swing.

3. The Counter: This student counts each period (back and forth swing) of the pendulum.

4. The Mathematician: This student converts the swings of the pendulum from periods/20 seconds to periods/minute.

After the students conduct the experiment and have recorded their data, use the class activity sheet to record each of the group's results and find the class average (mean). At this point, students can be asked to predict what will happen if the rope were 5 cm or 100 cm or if they believe that other variables might affect the cycles of the pendulum besides its length.

Assessment:

1. Student products: Data collected and recorded on the student activity sheet

2. Journal question: "Describe the pendulum experiment. Explain the procedures you used and briefly describe your results. Can you explain how this experiment relates to both scientific principles and mathematical statistics?"

Extension Activities or Projects:

This experiment can be repeated using pendulums of the same length but using weights of different mass or different angles. By extending the lesson using these variables, students will better understand that the mass or angle measurement has no effect on the period or swings of the pendulum.

Swings of the Pendulum—Selected Answers:

Answers will vary since they are based upon students' measurements.

Swings of the Pendulum

Name _____

Date _____ Class _____

Have you ever read Edgar Allan Poe's *The Pit and the Pendulum?* It's a real thriller about a man waiting for a sword at the end of a pendulum to do great harm to his body. Studying the science of pendulums is a good example of how math is used in the real world. Do you think the length of the rope has an effect on the number of times the pendulum swings back and forth (its period)? Let's conduct an experiment and see what effect, if any, the length of the rope attached to a weight has on the frequency of the pendulum in cycles/min.

Directions: Measure four lengths of string—25, 50, 100, and 150 cm. Attach each piece of string to a weight and work with your group to count the number of swings or cycles the pendulum makes per minute. Record your results on the Group Data Table below. When we compare your group's results with the rest of the class, using the Class Data Table (p. 46), we can analyze our results using the average number of periods (back and forth swings) per minute.

Swings of the Pendulum—Group Data Table

Length of String (in cm)	Periods (per 20 sec.)	Periods (per 1 min.)
25		
50		
100		
150		

Based upon your observations, what you can tell us about the relationship between the length of the rope and the period of the swings?

Swings of the Pendulum

Swings of the Pendulum—Class Data Table

Group	Number of Periods/Min. for Various Pendulum Lengths			
	25 cm	50 cm	100 cm	150 cm
1				
2				
3				
4				
5				
6				
7				
8				
9				
Mean				

Does there appear to be a relationship between the length of the pendulum and the number of periods per minute?

Swings of the Pendulum Journal Entry

Name _____

Date _____ Class _____

Use this page to explain the results of this experiment. Be sure to describe (1) what procedures you used to get your results, and (2) how your results compared to the data collected by other groups. The time it takes for a pendulum to swing to one side and back (its period in seconds) is related to its length. The formula is: $P = 1.1\sqrt{l}$

How did your results compare to this formula?

_____

_____

_____

_____

_____

_____

_____

_____

_____

_____

_____

ROLLER COASTERS: HOW FAST ARE WE FALLING?

Teacher's Planning Information

Background Information and Procedures:

A first glance at a roller coaster gives one the impression that it is a passenger train because it looks like a series of connected cars that move on a track. But unlike a typical train, a roller coaster has no engine or power source of its own. For most of the ride, only the forces of inertia and gravity move a roller coaster. At the beginning of the ride, the coaster train is pulled up the first hill, called the *lift hill.* The purpose of this initial ascent is to build up a reservoir of *potential energy* (stored energy). This energy is then released as *kinetic energy*—the energy of motion that takes the cars down the hill. A roller coaster's energy is constantly changing between potential and kinetic energy—the physics of force and motion.

The student worksheet, "How Fast Are We Falling? The Biggest Drops" (p. 51) has a table of the 11 roller coasters with the biggest drop. Students are asked to calculate the time it would take each of these coasters to fall from its highest point back to Earth. Discuss with students that because of the pull of gravity on the Earth—assuming there is no resistance such as air resistance or friction—all objects will speed up at a rate of 9.8 m/sec^2 for every second they fall. That is a speed increase of about 32 ft/sec^2 for every second the object falls. If we use the metric rate of acceleration, we can round the rate to 10 m/sec^2 and approximate the amount of time $D = \frac{1}{2}10t^2$ or $D = 5t^2$ it would take each of these mega–roller coasters to reach the earth. The distance an object falls on Earth is found by solving for t in the following formula: $t = \sqrt{\dfrac{D}{5}}$

Mathematical Connections:
Data collection, algebra, substitution for a variable, medians, box-and-whisker plots, radicals, graphing

Other Curricular Connections:
Physics, geography

Concepts:
Students will:

- Substitute distance into the acceleration formula to calculate the time it takes to get to the bottom of a vertical drop of a roller coaster
- Find the square root of a number
- Learn to design a box-and-whisker plot
- Analyze the data presented on a box-and-whisker plot
- Graph the acceleration of their calculations for one of the roller coasters

Materials Needed:

- Worksheets from this section for each student
- Calculators (essential to the lesson)

On "How Fast Are We Falling? Box-and-Whisker Plot," students analyze the data that has been listed from least to greatest by finding the median (midpoint) of the data, then finding the median of the lower half and the upper half of the data and plotting these on a number line. Specific directions are given in the lesson. This is an interesting graphic representation because each of the sections represents the same amount of data (25%), regardless of its size. The larger the quadrant, the greater the range of the data; the smaller the quadrant, the smaller the range of the data.

The final activity asks students to choose one of the roller coasters from the table and graph its decline in units of 0.25 seconds. This graph dramatically shows how this type of data produces a curve rather than a straight line.

Assessment:

1. Calculations and correct answers on worksheets

2. Journal question: "Design a box-and-whisker plot using the following data:"

Data for Journal Question

Animal	Speed in mph
Cheetah	70
Pronghorn antelope	61
Lion	50
Gazelle	50
Springbok	50
Brown hare	45
Horse	43
Gray fox	42
Greyhound	42
Rabbit	35
Kangaroo	30
Human	28
Black mamba snake	20
Pig (domestic)	11
Chicken	9

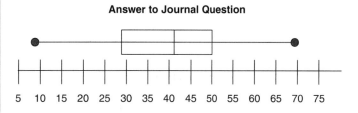

Answer to Journal Question

Roller Coasters—Selected Answers:

How Fast Are We Falling? The Biggest Drops: These answers have been rounded to the nearest tenth.

Answers to student data table

Coaster	Location	Drop (in meters)	Year Built	Falling Time $t = \sqrt{\frac{d}{5}}$
Kingda Ka	New Jersey	127	2005	5.0 sec.
Top Thriller Dragster	Ohio	122	2003	4.9 sec.
Superman: The Escape & Tower of Terror	California & Queensland, Australia	100	1997 &1997	4.5 sec.
Steel Dragon	Nagashima Mie, Japan	94	2000	4.3 sec.
Millennium Force	Ohio	91	2000	4.3 sec.
Titan & Goliath	Texas & California	78	2001 & 2000	3.9 sec.
Fujiyama	Yamanashi, Japan	70	1996	3.7 sec.
Phantom's Revenge	Pennsylvania	69	2001	3.7 sec.
Son of Beast	Ohio	65	2000	3.7 sec.
El Toro	New Jersey	54	2006	3.6 sec.
Colossos	Niedersachsen, Germany	48	2001	3.3 sec.

Source: http://www.coastergrotto.com/biggest-roller-coasters.jsp

How Fast Are We Falling? Box-and-Whisker Plot

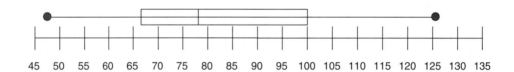

45 50 55 60 65 70 75 80 85 90 95 100 105 110 115 120 125 130 135

1. The median of the set of data is 78.

2. The median of the lower quartile is 67.

3. The median of the upper quartile is 100.

4. 25 percent of the data falls within each quartile.

5. 50 percent of the data falls within the box.

6. The range of the data in each of the quartiles is different. For example, in the first quartile, the range is between 48 and 67—a difference of 19. But in the second quartile, the range is between 67 and 78—a range of only 11—so the size of the box is smaller. Students can calculate the range of each of the quartiles and compare their areas.

How Fast Are We Falling? Our Acceleration Graph

1. The units used on the graphs will vary based upon the roller coaster students choose to use. However, each of the graphs will be a downward curve.

How Fast Are We Falling?
The Biggest Drops

Name _____

Date _____ Class _____

On Earth, objects accelerate at a speed of 10 m/sec². The distance something travels can be computed using this formula: Distance = 1/2 Acceleration × Time² or $D = 1/2\ 10t^2$.

Since A = 10 m/sec², the formula can be simplified to $D = 5t^2$.

When we solve for t, the formula becomes: $t = \sqrt{\dfrac{d}{5}}$

The highest drop for these roller coasters will be considered a *vertical drop*. Since the roller coasters are not completely vertical, it will take them a little bit longer to reach the bottom.

Coaster	Location	Vertical Drop (in meters)	Year Built	Falling Time $t = \sqrt{\dfrac{d}{5}}$
Kingda Ka	New Jersey	127	2005	
Top Thriller Dragster	Ohio	122	2003	
Superman: The Escape & Tower of Terror	California & Queensland, Australia	100	1997 & 1997	
Steel Dragon	Nagashima Mie, Japan	94	2000	
Millennium Force	Ohio	91	2000	
Titan & Goliath	Texas & California	78	2001 & 2000	
Fujiyama	Yamanashi, Japan	70	1996	
Phantom's Revenge	Pennsylvania	69	2001	
Son of Beast	Ohio	65	2000	
El Toro	New Jersey	54	2006	
Colossos	Niedersachsen, Germany	48	2001	

Source: http://www.coastergrotto.com/biggest-roller-coasters.jsp

How Fast Are We Falling?
Box-and-Whisker Plot

Name _____

Date _____ Class _____

These numbers show the roller coaster drops from "How Fast Are We Falling? The Biggest Drop."

48,   54,   65,   69,   70,   78,   78,   91,   94,   100,   100,   122,   127

Why does the list include two 78s and two 100s? _____

To design the box-and-whisker plot, follow the steps below:

1. Find the median number (the number that is in the middle) for the group of numbers above. The median number for this data is _____. Circle that number.

2. Next find the median of the lower half of the data. The median for the lower half of the data is _____. Circle that number.

3. Next, find the median of the upper half of the data: The median for the upper half of the data is _____. Circle that number.

The shortest and longest drops have been labeled on the graph. These are called the *whiskers*. Using these whiskers as your guide, draw a box that represents the three quartiles.

45 50 55 60 65 70 75 80 85 90 95 100 105 110 115 120 125 130 135

4. What percentage of the data falls in each of the quartiles? _____

5. What percentage of the data falls inside the box? _____

6. Although the same number of roller coasters is represented in each quartile, they are not the same size. How do you explain this?

How Fast Are We Falling?
Our Acceleration Graph

Name _____

Date _____ Class _____

Choose one of the roller coasters from the list of "The Biggest Drops" and graph the relationship between the time it takes you to fall and the distance you have traveled. Remember the formula is $D = 5t^2$. Be sure to use equal units when you label your axes. The vertical axis represents the distance the roller coaster falls, and the horizontal axis represents time (in seconds).

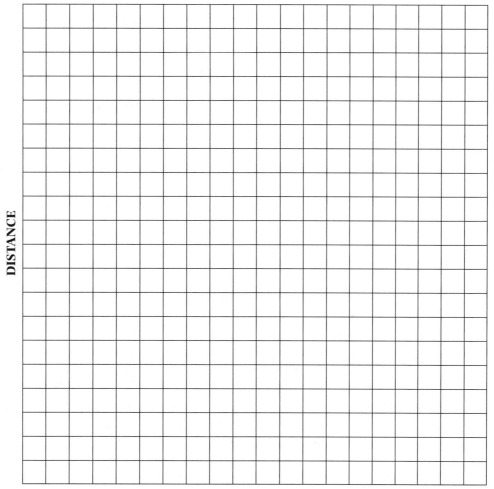

DISTANCE

TIME (in seconds)

ADDITIONAL READING

Density and Other Science

Chahrour, J. P. (2000) *Flash! Bang! Fizz! Exciting science for curious minds.* Hauppauge, NY: Barron's Educational Series.

> Presents the procedures and concepts involved in 25 physical science experiments that can be done at home with readily available materials, exploring gases, density, fluid dynamics, gravity, and motion.

De Pree, C. (2004). *Physics made simple.* New York: Broadway Books.

> A completely revised edition of a 1989 book, introduces students to a nonthreatening look at physics of the everyday world.

Pendulums

Enderle, D. (2005). *The burning pendulum.* St. Paul, MN: Llewellyn.

> In a book report, Juniper mentions fortune telling and has caused a real problem at school. All she did was describe her favorite book and demonstrate how to use a pendulum, but not everyone thinks fortune telling is an appropriate topic. Juniper is in danger of being suspended from school, so her friends call an emergency meeting of the Fortune Tellers Club to see how they can help. Can a mysterious clue help clear Juniper's name?

Robertson, W. C. (2002). *Force and motion: Stop faking it! Finally understanding science so you can teach it.* Arlington, VA: NSTA.

> The book's seven chapters combine easy-to-understand explanations of Newton's laws of motion with activities using commonly found equipment.

Roller Coasters

Bennett, D. (1998). *Roller coaster: Wooden and steel coasters, twisters, and corkscrews.* New York: Book Sales.

> Although this book is a few years old, it is one of the better reference books for students to use. The book is divided into five chapters: (1) the history of coasters, (2) the engineering behind them, (3) biographical information of some of the more famous designers, (4) information about amusement parks, and (5) information about some of the greatest thrill rides throughout history.

Breaux, S. (2002). *Sudden turn.* New York: Penguin Putnam Books for Young Readers.

> This is the first book of the *Roller Coaster Tycoon* series, mysteries written for students ages 8 to 12. These books tell the story of brother and sister Marty and Magnolia Butterfield who have inherited a great deal of money and have decided to use their inheritance to build their own amusement parks. The other books in the series, written between 2002 and 2005, are *Sabotage* by Shane Breaux, *The Great Coaster Contest* by Tracey West, *Kidnapped* by Larry M. Garmon, *Haunted Parkway* by Katherine Noll, and *Spaced Out* by Bobbi Weiss.

INTERNET WEB SITES

http://eserver.org/books/poe/pit_and_the_pendulum.html

The Pit and the Pendulum was written by Edgar Allan Poe in 1842—it is available at this Web site as an online version.

http://www.learner.org/exhibits/parkphysics/coaster/

Students design their own roller coaster! They are asked to choose the height and shape of the first hill, the slope of the hills and the shape of the loops. At the end of the design process, their roller coaster is rated, thumbs up or thumbs down, on two criteria—safety and fun. The student designers are told why they received their ratings and are given an opportunity to try again if their first designs were not successful.

http://science.howstuffworks.com/roller~coaster2.htm

This site gives students the opportunity to visualize how the initial lift-hill in a roller coaster serves to build up potential energy and the relationship between potential and kinetic energy at various spots on the roller coaster.

http://www.funderstanding.com/k12/coaster/

Another site where students design their own roller coaster but this time students set the height of the first and second hills, the size of the loop, the initial speed of the coaster, its mass, the gravity at work, and the amount of friction on the track. Then the roller coaster tries to run from the beginning of the track to the end without running into any problems!

Our Body Systems, Forensics, and Math

3

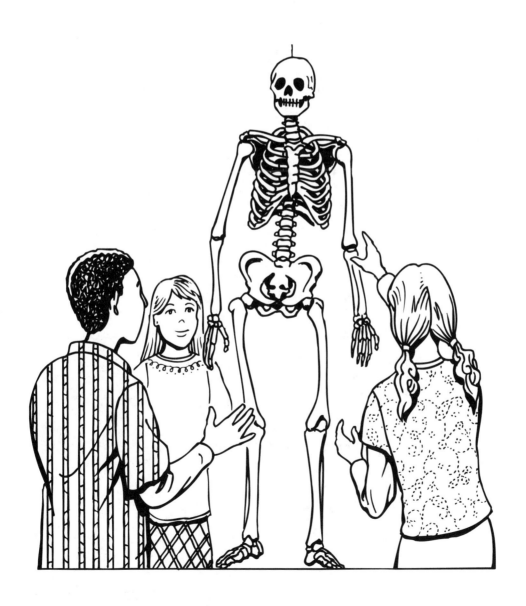

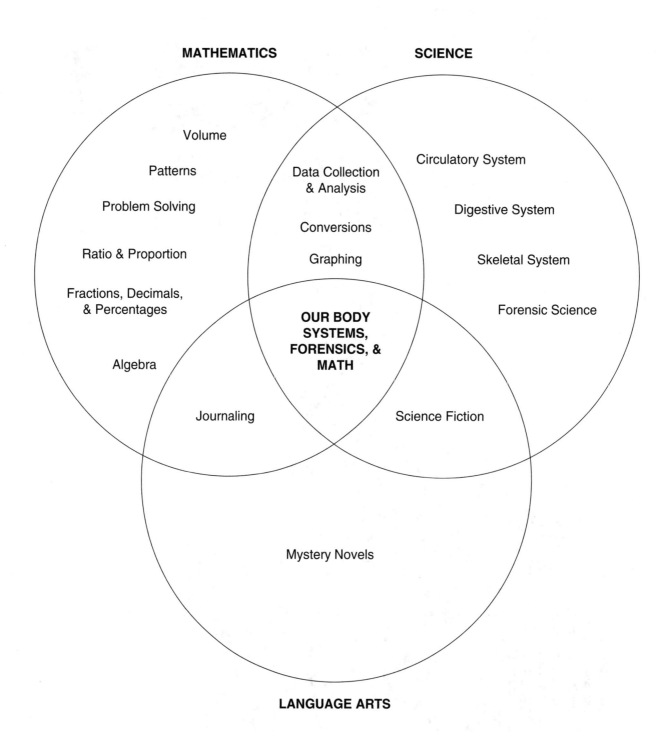

MATHEMATICS

SCIENCE

Volume

Patterns

Problem Solving

Ratio & Proportion

Fractions, Decimals,
& Percentages

Algebra

Data Collection
& Analysis

Conversions

Graphing

Circulatory System

Digestive System

Skeletal System

Forensic Science

**OUR BODY
SYSTEMS,
FORENSICS, &
MATH**

Journaling

Science Fiction

Mystery Novels

LANGUAGE ARTS

Our Body 3 Systems, Forensics, and Math

Mathematics is the science which draws necessary conclusions.

—Benjamin Peirce (1809–1880)

INTRODUCTION

In this chapter, we look at motivating real-world connections between mathematics and science. In mathematics, students focus on measurement, ratios and proportions, fractions, decimals, data collection and analysis, problem solving, and percentages. The connections to science made in this chapter start with a brief glimpse of the circulatory, digestive, and skeletal systems, and end with three activities related to forensic science.

In the section called "Our Remarkable Heart," students learn that the heart is, in fact, a remarkable organ! In three different activities, students compute how many times their heart beats when at rest, how its beat changes during exercise, and how many gallons of blood it pumps each day (more or less than a bathtub full).

The digestive system is another remarkable feat of engineering. It has been called a "disassembly line" because of the way it takes food and breaks it down rather than putting it together. "The Sum of the Parts: How Long Is Your Digestive System?" introduces students to the eleven major parts, starting at the mouth and ending at the anus. Working in pairs, students learn about this remarkable organ system.

Forensic science has become enormously popular in recent years. *Crime Scene Investigation (CSI)* television shows that take place in Las Vegas, Miami, and New York demonstrate how precise measurements, mathematics, and science help police solve crimes. The first of three lessons related to forensics is a hands-on experiment titled "Find Your Body's Ratios." Students collect two pieces of data about each person in their group: their total height and the length of their left foot. When ratios, proportions, and percentages are employed, students learn how forensic anthropologists make predictions about crime victims.

The amazing ratios found in our body are highlighted again in the second lesson in this section, "Forensics and the Human Skeleton." Students learn how forensic scientists can approximate the height of victims by using formulas developed by studying the body ratios of thousands of people. After taking their own bone measurements, students compare their actual heights to calculated heights, using formulas.

The last activity related to forensics is "Fingerprints: A Unique Classification." Working in groups, students identify their own fingerprints, collect class data, and analyze and graph their results. Students can discuss how the class sample might compare to the population as a whole.

At the end of the chapter, the list of books included in "Additional Reading" contain both fiction and nonfiction books. Perhaps the language arts teacher could include some of them on his or her reading list.

OUR REMARKABLE HEART

Teacher's Planning Information

Background Information and Procedures:

There are three different experiments in this lesson. The first experiment, "How Many Beats?", encourages students to find their average heart rate. After recording the number of times their heart beats in 15 seconds, they convert this measurement to beats per minute, beats per day, and finally, beats per year. Explain that accurate measurements are very important since the data obtained using a very short interval of time will be used to make estimations for a much longer period of time—from how many beats in 15 seconds to how many in a year. This type of prediction requires the initial measurement to be as accurate as possible because any error will be multiplied many times over when it is expanded. This phenomenon, known as *sensitive dependence on initial conditions*—a part of chaos theory—states that just a small change in the initial conditions of a problem can drastically change the final answer when working on a large series of calculations. This type of discussion with students helps them understand why we should not round our answers at each step of a problem but instead wait for the final answer to do any rounding.

The second experiment examines the difference in heart rates when the body is at rest as opposed to during exercise. After students have found their heart rate at rest, they are asked to exercise and then compare the two rates. Again, precise timing and measurement is the key to success.

The third and final experiment, finding the volume of a bathtub, is an open-ended problem. The average bathtub has a volume of about 45 cubic feet of water, but there is great variance in

Mathematical Connections:
Data collection and analysis, volume, conversions, problem solving

Other Curricular Connections:
Circulatory system, literature

Concepts:
Students will:

- Collect data to compute their heart rates
- Compute the volume of blood that flows through their body in one day
- Problem-solve the relationship between the volume of their bathtub and the volume of blood pumped in one day
- Collect data and compute the increase in heart rate during exercise

Materials Needed:
- Watches with second hands
- Copies of worksheets (1) "How Many Beats?" (2) "How Much Blood?" and (3) "How Fast Does Your Heart Beat?" for each group of students
- Calculators

size (depending on the type of tub the student has). There are many ways students can find an approximate volume. Again, discuss the importance of careful planning. How can we measure a large quantity of water? An interesting problem!

Once the experiments are complete, bring the groups together to discuss the average heart rate, the rate of flow, how the heart rate is affected by exercise, how much water a bathtub holds, and how that volume relates to the amount of blood that travels through the body in one day.

Assessment:

1. Student products—Accurate calculations and worthwhile discussion on student worksheets

2. Journal question: "Discuss what you learned about your heart rate and volume of blood from your experiments."

Our Remarkable Heart—Selected Answers:

How Many Beats? While student answers will depend upon data collected in groups, the average heart rate of someone at rest is about 72 beats per minute.

How Fast Does Your Heart Beat? Answers will vary.

How Much Blood? (1) 15,750 gallons of blood; (2) Answers will vary based upon the size of the bathtub, but since most bathtubs hold about 45 gallons, the heart pumps about 350 times more blood than the volume of the average bathtub.

How Many Beats?

Name _____

Date _____ Class _____

Imagine a pump (about the size of a clenched fist) that weighs about half a pound and works 24 hours a day for 70 years or more! It has the power of a champion athlete and has enough energy to raise a small car off the ground. This remarkable pump is the human heart!

The heart is the body's key to survival. It pumps blood carrying a supply of food and oxygen to billions of cells and carries carbon dioxide and other wastes away from the cells. What a hard worker! But just how hard does it work? These activities will help us better understand our remarkable heart.

How many times per minute do you think your heart beats? How many times do you think your heart beats in one day? In one year? Work with your group to find your mean (or average) heart rate.

How Many Beats?—Group Data Table

Your Name	Beats per 15 seconds	Beats per Minute	Beats per Day	Beats per Year

The average life expectancy in the United States in 2005 was 77 years and 5 months. Work with your group to compute how many times a heart will beat in 77 years and 5 months. Explain how you solved this problem on the back of this paper.

How Fast Does Your Heart Beat?

Name _____

Date _____ Class _____

The healthy heart of an adult at rest beats about 72 times each minute, but the normal range is between 60 and 100. What was the mean at-rest heart rate for your group?

However, physical exertion elevates our pulse rate. How do you think your heart rate might vary with exercise?

Let's work in groups to conduct an experiment to help answer this question.

Directions: Work with your group to find the average heart rate while exercising.

Running in Place for 1 Minute		
Your Name	*Beats per 15 Seconds*	*Beats per 1 Minute*
Mean		

Jumping in Place for 1 Minute		
Your Name	*Beats per 15 Seconds*	*Beats per 1 Minute*
Mean		

How was your group's heart rate affected by exercise? _____

_____

_____

_____

_____

_____

_____

_____

_____

How Much Blood?

Name _____

Date _____ Class _____

The average amount of blood pumped by the heart with each beat is about 5 ounces.

An adult heart beats at an average of 70 beats per minute or about 100,800 beats each day!

Use this information to compute the number of gallons of blood pumped every day through our blood vessels. The facts on this conversion table will help you with your computation:

> 8 ounces = 1 cup
>
> 2 cups = 1 pint (16 oz)
>
> 2 pints = 1 quart (32 oz)
>
> 4 quarts = 1 gallon (128 oz)

1. How many gallons of blood does your heart pump? Use this space to explain your reasoning:

    Next find out the following:

    How much water does your bathtub hold?

2. Your assignment tonight is to calculate the volume of water it would take to fill your bathtub. How does this volume compare to the amount of blood your heart pumps in one day? Explain how you (1) found the volume of water your bathtub would hold and (2) how it compares to the amount of blood your heart pumps in one day. Write your answers on the back of this paper.

THE SUM OF THE PARTS: HOW LONG IS YOUR DIGESTIVE SYSTEM?

Teacher's Planning Information

Background Information and Procedures:

Ask students how long they think their digestive systems are. Remind them that the digestive system starts at the mouth. Give students a chance to discuss this, then write their answers down so they can be referred to at a later time. Give each pair of students a copy of the "Sum of the Parts: How Long Is Your Digestive System?" worksheet. Go over the procedures with students; make sure that students understand the locations and sizes to be measured. Each measurement must be entered on the sheet before they move on.

Have each group get the supplies they need and then begin collecting data. For the class record sheet, you will need the heights of each student in the class. Remind students that their height must be measured in centimeters and included with the digestive system's measurements.

When individual groups have finished collecting their data, have them write their mean lengths on the "How Long Is Your Digestive System?—Class Data Table" as well as the mean heights of the individuals in their group. By dividing the length of their digestive system by their mean height, a decimal ratio is calculated. The length of the small and large intestines is five times a person's height, but a little more should be added for the mouth, esophagus, and stomach.

Mathematical Connections:
Measurement, data collection and analysis

Other Curricular Connections:
Digestive system

Concepts:
Students will:

- Measure using a nontraditional instrument, then interpret that distance using metric measurements
- Calculate mean lengths
- Find the relationship between the length of their digestive system and their total height

Materials Needed:
- String (about 8 meters or 26 feet per group)
- A copy of student worksheet, "The Sum of the Parts: How Long Is Your Digestive System?" for each pair of students
- Overhead transparency of "How Long Is Your Digestive System?—Class Data Table"
- Meter sticks or tape measures
- Calculators

Assessment:

1. Accuracy of measurements and written response on student worksheet

2. Journal question: "What relationship, if any, did you find between the length of the digestive system and the mean height of the students in your class? Do you think this number could be used to predict the height of a person if you knew the length of the digestive system? Why or why not?"

Sum of the Parts: How Long Is Your Digestive System?—Selected Answers:

Answers will vary for measurements, but the length of the digestive system is a little bit more than five times a person's height.

The Sum of the Parts: How Long Is Your Digestive System?

Name _____

Date _____ Class _____

Directions: You will work with a partner on this activity.

1. Before you begin, find each of your heights (measured to the nearest centimeter). Enter these measurements on the table.

2. Now make the measurements listed in the table using a length of string about 9 meters long. After each measurement, tie a knot, *but do not cut the string!* The next measurement is taken from the last knot on the long string.

3. You will record each measurement on the table by measuring the length of the string between the knot you have just made and the one that preceded it. Be sure to enter each measurement on the data table each time. The total length of the system is *the sum of the parts.*

4. Round each answer to the nearest centimeter. Find the mean length of each measurement.

Your Name	Your Height	Mouth to Back of Jaw (Mouth)	Back of Jaw to Bottom of Sternum (Esophagus)	Thumb to Pinkie (Stomach)	4 × Your Height (Small Intestines)	1 × Your Height (Large Intestines)	Total Length of System
Mean							

Share your data with some of the other groups. Describe (analyze) your results. Be sure to include any relationships that you see between your height and the length of the system:

The Sum of the Parts: How Long Is Your Digestive System?

How Long Is Your Digestive System?—Class Data Table

Group	Mean Length of Digestive System	Mean Height of Group Members	Mean Length of System ÷ Mean Height
Class Mean			

Does there appear to be a relationship between a person's height and the length of his or her digestive system?

FIND YOUR BODY'S RATIOS

Teacher's Planning Information

Background Information and Procedures:

Mathematical Connections:
Measurement, ratio and proportion, fractions, decimals

Other Curricular Connections:
Human anatomy, forensic anthropology

Concepts:
Students will:

- Measure their height
- Measure the length of their right foot from the wall to their big toe
- Find the ratio of the two measurements
- Calculate a class mean
- Use the mean to form a conjecture to describe the relationship between a person's height and his or her foot measurement

Materials Needed:

- Tape measures or meter sticks
- Copy of "Find Your Body's Ratios" worksheet for each group of students
- Overhead transparency of "Find Your Body's Ratios—Class Data Table" worksheet

Ask students how they think forensic pathologists can estimate the height of a victim when only a foot is available for measurement. Discuss a possible mathematical relationship or ratio between the two lengths. They might wish to consider whether a 7-foot basketball player might have the same size foot as a 5-foot ballerina—and why or why not!

Individual groups will be measuring their height and foot lengths, but for the class mean to have validity, it is important for students to discuss and agree on procedures that each group must use when making their measurements. Suggest that students remove their shoes before measuring their height (different types of shoes will affect their measurements) and measure the length of their right or left foot from the wall to the tip of their big toe. (Since our feet are not the same size, it is important that the same foot be measured for each student.)

The class mean can be converted to a percentage and this can be used to predict a person's height (when the person's foot length is known) and vice versa.

Assessment:

1. Data collection and computation on student worksheets

2. Journal question: "The ratio between a person's height and the measurement from his or her waist to the top of the head is 2:5. Explain how this ratio can be used by forensic pathologists."

Find Your Body's Ratios—Selected Answers:

Answers will vary but the average ratio between foot size and height is about 3:20. An adult's foot size is about 15% of his or her total height.

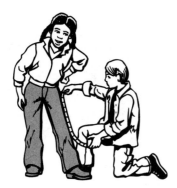

Find Your Body's Ratios

Name _____

Date _____ Class _____

Directions: Work with your group to do the following:

1. Without shoes, accurately measure your total height.

2. Measure the length of the agreed-upon foot from the wall to the tip of the big toe.

3. Set up a ratio of $\dfrac{\text{length of foot}}{\text{total height}}$

4. Convert the fractional ratio to a decimal.

5. Record your data on the table and find the group's mean.

Name	Length of Foot	Total Height	Ratio $\dfrac{\text{length of foot}}{\text{total height}}$	Decimal
Mean				

6. Using your group's means, find the approximate percentage of the group's height represented by the length of the group's foot. The percentage is _____

7. Is this percentage the same for each of the group's members? Why or why not? Write your answer on the back of this paper.

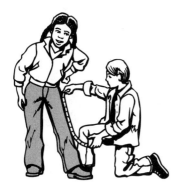

Find Your Body's Ratios

Find Your Body's Ratios—Class Data Table

Group	Decimal Ratio	Precentage
A		
B		
C		
D		
E		
F		
G		
H		
Class Mean		

Now share your data with the other groups on the "Find Your Body's Ratios—Class Data Table."

Explain any relationship you see between a person's height and the length of the person's foot—does there appear to be a constant ratio between these two measurements?

FORENSICS AND THE HUMAN SKELETON

Teacher's Planning Information

Background Information and Procedures:

Discuss with students how knowing the physical dimensions of a crime victim can greatly help law enforcement officials identify that victim. When a skeleton is found, a forensic scientist can use the lengths of certain bones to calculate the height of the victim. The bones that can be used are the femur, the tibia, the humerus, and the radius. There are different formulas used for males and females. While only two bones are used in this experiment, the table below shows the formulas for each of the bones listed above:

The variables represented by capital letters in each of the formulas shown below should be replaced by the student's bone measurement. The tibia and the humerus are used in this experiment because they are easy to find and measure. The other two bones can be used as an extension activity or to collect additional data if necessary.

It is important to note that after the age of 30, the height of a person begins to decrease at a rate of approximately 0.06 cm per year. If the age of the victim can be determined by another method, the amount of shrinkage must be considered when figuring the person's height.

After groups have finished collecting their data and calculating their heights, each student should enter his or her name on the "Forensics and the Human Skeleton—Class Data Table" along with the student's actual height, the bone measurement/height calculation that was the more accurate of the two, and the percentage of error between the two. The class then calculates an average percentage of error.

If the calculations obtained from bone measurements are inaccurate, students can discuss why they

Mathematical Connections:
Metric measurement, using formulas, rational numbers, percent of error, data collection and analysis

Other Curricular Connections:
Forensic science

Concepts:
Students will:

- Measure their height in centimeters
- Measure their tibia and humerus bones
- Apply formulas to calculate their approximate height
- Analyze data to calculate percentage of error

Materials Needed:
- One tape measure and meter stick per group
- Group data collection sheet— "Forensics and the Human Skeleton"
- Calculators
- Overhead transparency of "Forensics and the Human Skeleton—Class Data Table"

Height Formulas

Name of Bone	Formula (male)	Formula (female)
Femur	h = 69.089 + 2.238F	h = 61.412 + 2.317F
Tibia	h = 81.688 + 2.392T	h = 72.572 + 2.533T
Humerus	h = 73.570 + 2.970H	h = 64.977 + 3.144H
Radius	h = 80.405 + 3.650R	h = 73.502 + 3.876R

believe this occurred. Sometimes inaccuracies occur because bones were not measured properly or their exact placement (between joints) was incorrect. If measurements are redone, it is sometimes easier to fine the joints separating the bones by moving the arm or the leg and locating the joints before taking the measurement.

Assessment:

Journal question: "If it is determined that the victim was a 63-year-old female and the tibia measured 33.7 cm, what was the woman's height? (A person shrinks approximately 0.06 cm each year over the age of 30.)" [Answer: Approx. 156 cm]

Forensics and the Human Skeleton—Selected Answers:

Answers depend on measurements.

Forensics and the Human Skeleton

Name _____

Date _____ Class _____

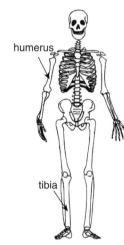

humerus

tibia

Forensic scientists can use the size of a victim's bones to help them estimate the actual height of the person. For example: by measuring the tibia or the humerus bones and entering these measurements into a formula, scientists can determine the height of the living person. This can help in the identification process. Today we are going to conduct some experiments that are like those conducted by forensic scientists.

Directions: You will be working in groups of four for this activity.

1. Measure each group member's height to the nearest centimeter.

2. Then measure the tibia bone (T) of each member of the group and enter it in the correct column (male or female) on the data collection table.

3. Use the appropriate formula to calculate the height of the person.

4. Repeat the experiment using the humerus bone (H). You may use the actual height used in the first experiment.

Measurement using the Tibia bone (in the leg). All measurements are in cm.						
Name of Person	Length of Bone	Male Formula: h=81.688 + 2.392T	Female Formula: h=72.572 + 2.533T	Calculated Height (Using formula)	Actual Height (Measured)	% of Error

Measurement using the Tibia bone (in the leg). All measurements are in cm.						
Name of Person	Length of Bone	Male Formula: h = 73.570 + 2.970H	Female Formula: h = 64.977 + 3.144H	Calculated Height (Using formula)	Actual Height (Measured)	% of Error

Did one of the bone measurements give a more accurate approximation of the actual height than the other? If it did, why do you think this occurred? Let's use class data to find the average percentage of error.

Forensics and the Human Skeleton

Forensics and the Human Skeleton—Class Data Table

Name	Height Using Formula (Most accurate one)	Actual Height	% of Error
Average % of Error			

FINGERPRINTS: A UNIQUE CLASSIFICATION

Teacher's Planning Information

Background Information and Procedures:

Give each group the packet of worksheets that includes fingerprint types and the grid each group will use to place their thumbprints. Discuss the various types of fingerprints and what characteristics place them in a particular category. Make sure that students understand that they are to identify their type of fingerprint and place it into one of the three major categories—loop, arch, or whorl. For the purposes of this activity, variations of fingerprint types will be included in the larger category. Examples of each type are shown on the students' worksheet pages along with descriptions.

When each group has completed their portion of the data collection, have each person shade in the appropriate section on the class data table. Use this graph to complete the frequency table at the bottom of the page that asks for number of students, fraction of students, and percentage. The percentage that each category can be found in the general population is shown on the table as well. Discuss with students how the class percentages compare with those of the rest of the population. Percentages of difference can be calculated for each category.

Students use the percentages from this frequency table to complete an individual circle graph of the data. This individual project can be included in the assessment process.

Mathematical Connections:
Data collection and analysis, percentages, circle graphs, pattern observation

Other Curricular Connections:
Forensic science

Concepts:
Students will:

- Work in a group of four and take a thumbprint of each member
- Use the samples provided to analyze each print and classify it in one of three major categories
- Combine individual group data and use class data to analyze percentages
- Measure and design a circle graph of class data

Materials Needed:
- Worksheet packet for each group
- One circle graph sheet for each student
- One index card per group of four
- One soft pencil for each group
- Scotch tape for each group
- Protractors, rulers, and colored pencils for graph

Suggestions for Assessment:

1. Accuracy of data on group data collection sheets

2. Individual circle graphs

3. Journal question: "Explain how the data collected by the class compares to the percentages of fingerprint types in the greater population. What was the percentage of difference between class data and actual occurrence of fingerprint type?"

Fingerprints: A Unique Classification—Selected Answers:

Answers will vary but if the percentage of students is similar to those of the population, the graph will look like this:

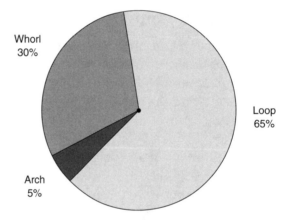

Whorl 30%

Loop 65%

Arch 5%

Fingerprints: A Unique Classification

Name _____

Date _____ Class _____

While fingerprints appeared on prehistoric drawings, it was in fourteenth-century Persia that official government papers were first noted to have fingerprints (impressions), and one doctor observed that no two fingerprints were exactly alike. It was not until 1941 that fingerprints were accepted as evidence in court. Up to that time, it was not an established fact that no two fingerprints are alike. Forensic scientists use these types of fingerprints to help identify unknown people:

Loops (about 65% of all fingerprints): There are two patterns of loops: the ulnar and the radial. In these two patterns, the ridges enter from one side of the finger, curve to form a loop, and then exit on the same side.

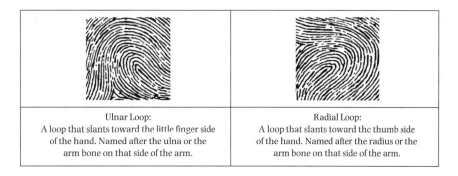

Ulnar Loop: A loop that slants toward the little finger side of the hand. Named after the ulna or the arm bone on that side of the arm.	Radial Loop: A loop that slants toward the thumb side of the hand. Named after the radius or the arm bone on that side of the arm.

Arches (about 5% of all fingerprints): There are two types of arch fingerprints; the first is a tented arch and the second is the plain arch. Both enter the finger from one side, flow smoothly to form what appears to be a hill, and then exit on the opposite side of the finger.

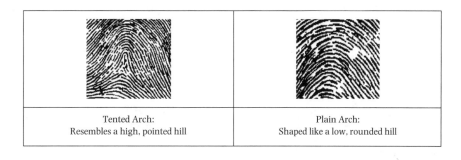

Tented Arch: Resembles a high, pointed hill	Plain Arch: Shaped like a low, rounded hill

Whorls (about 30% of all fingerprints): There are four kinds of whorls—they are shown below. Two of the whorls have the word "loop" in their name, but this is because they do not enter and exit on the same side of the finger. The "Accidental Whorl" pattern may resemble some of the other patterns but not enough to be classified as one of the others. Also, this pattern tends to enter on one side and exit on the other side of the finger.

A Variety of Whorls

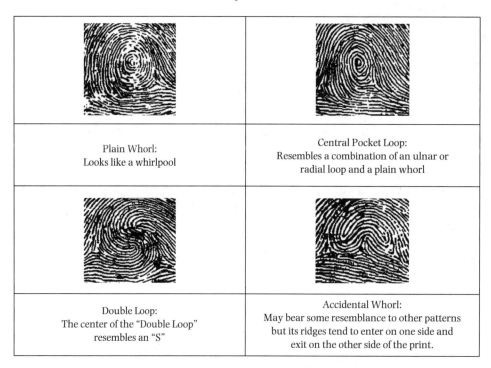

Plain Whorl: Looks like a whirlpool	Central Pocket Loop: Resembles a combination of an ulnar or radial loop and a plain whorl
Double Loop: The center of the "Double Loop" resembles an "S"	Accidental Whorl: May bear some resemblance to other patterns but its ridges tend to enter on one side and exit on the other side of the print.

Use these fingerprint types to help you identify the fingerprints of the members of your group. Although there are different types within each category, eventually they will be placed into three major category types: loop, arch, or whorl.

Fingerprints: A Unique Classification

Directions:

1. Use a soft pencil to cover an index card with graphite. Rub your thumb over the graphite on the card until your thumb is dark with graphite.

2. Carefully place your thumb on a small piece of scotch tape.

3. Then tape the fingerprint in the space provided next to your name on the data collection table.

4. Work with your group to identify the type of fingerprint you have.

5. Share your data with the rest of the groups on the class data table.

Fingerprints—Group Data Collection Table

Name	Fingerprint	Classification

Fingerprints:
A Unique Classification

Fingerprints—Class Data Table

Type	Students
Loop	
Arch	
Whorl	

Data Analysis—Class Data Table

Fingerprint Type	Number of Students	Fraction	Percent of Class	Percent of Population
Loop				65%
Arch				5%
Whorl				30%

How does our class compare to the rest of the population?

Fingerprints:
A Unique Classification

Name _____

Date _____ Class _____

Use the percentages from the class data to design this circle graph.

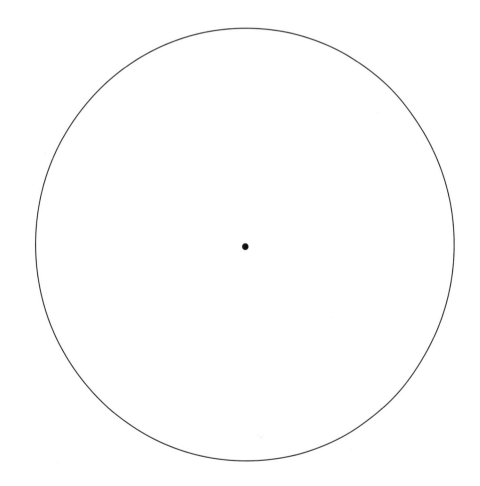

ADDITIONAL READING

Body Systems

Asimov, I. (Reissue version 1988). *Fantastic voyage.* New York: Bantam Books.

> This science fiction novel was originally released as a movie in 1966. It is about five people who are miniaturized and sent into the body of a scientist to try to destroy a blood clot in his brain.

Colombo, L., Zuckerman, C., & Fairman, J. (2003). *Uncover the human body.* Berkeley, CA: Silver Dolphin Books.

> This book takes some of the mysteries out of how the body works through hands-on exploration. Students get to look at each system on a different page, then by closing the book, combine them into a whole.

Lambourne, M. (1991). *Inside story.* Brookfield, CT: Millbrook Press.

> With a sense of humor, this book describes the workings of the human body, covering the major organ systems and health tips.

Simon, S. (2000). *Bones: Our skeletal system.* New York: HarperCollins.

> This book acquaints students with amazing facts about the 206 bones that make up their skeleton.

Wiese, J. (2000). *Head to toe science: Over 40 eye-popping, spine-tingling, heart-pounding activities that teach kids about the human body.* Arlington, VA: NSTA.

> This book contains 46 active projects to help students learn about the body's systems, including brain, circulatory, skeletal, and reproductive. It's written for students but organized to help teachers connect classroom experiments to real-life applications.

Forensics

Jackson, D. M. (1996). *Bone detectives: How forensic anthropologists solve crimes and uncover mysteries of the dead.* New York: Little, Brown.

> This book follows an actual murder investigation step-by-step. Students learn how forensic anthropologists can discover a person's vital statistics by studying his or her bones and teeth and how they use clay to reconstruct a face from a skull.

Oxlade, C. (2005). *Detective tool kit: Investigate everyday mysteries with forensic science.* Philadelphia: Running Press.

> This kit provides students with the tools they need to solve household mysteries. Using fingerprints, students can discover who drank the last glass of milk, or working with hair samples they can figure out whose hairbrush was left on the sink!

Platt, R. (2005). *Forensics.* New York: Houghton Mifflin.

> Students explore a crime lab and discover how detectives use science to solve crimes. This book relates how famous crimes were solved and how they were committed.

Science Mystery Books

Torrey, M. (2002). *Case of the gasping garbage.* New York: Penguin Putnam.

> First in the series of mysteries where fourth graders Drake Doyle and Neil Fossey combine detective and scientific investigation skills to solve mysteries.

Torrey, M. (2002). *Case of the graveyard ghost.* New York: Penguin Putnam.

> Now in fifth grade, this is the second in the series of Doyle and Fossey's investigations.

Torrey, M. (2003). *The case of the barfy birthday.* New York: Penguin Putnam.

> The third book in this series of elementary school-aged detectives who solve mysteries using their scientific skills.

Quilts, Tessellations, and Three-Dimensional Geometry

4

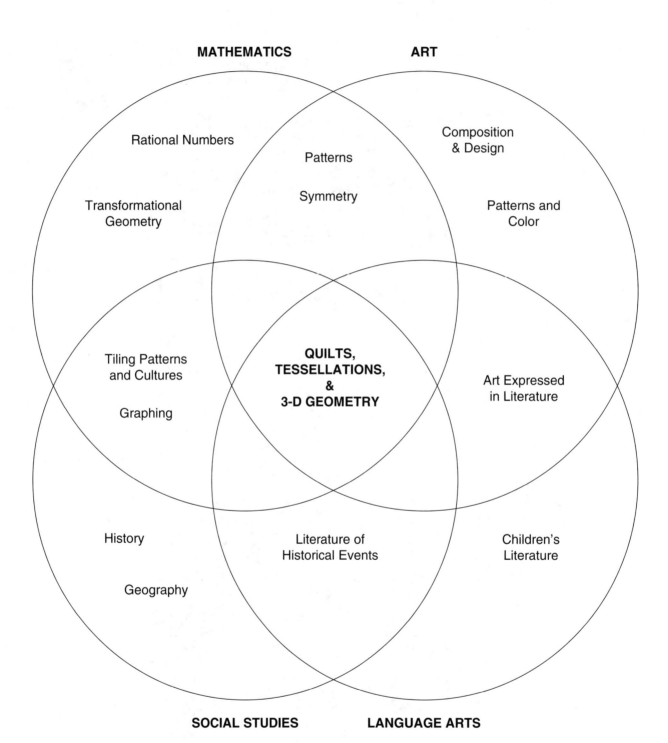

MATHEMATICS **ART**

Rational Numbers

Composition
& Design

Patterns

Symmetry

Patterns and
Color

Transformational
Geometry

Tiling Patterns
and Cultures

**QUILTS,
TESSELLATIONS,
&
3-D GEOMETRY**

Art Expressed
in Literature

Graphing

History

Literature of
Historical Events

Children's
Literature

Geography

SOCIAL STUDIES **LANGUAGE ARTS**

Quilts, Tessellations, and Three-Dimensional Geometry **4**

A good part of art is based upon geometry.

—Giraud Desargues

INTRODUCTION

It has been said that mathematics is the science of patterns and symmetry. That's not a bad description. Symmetry is all around us—there is symmetry in everyday objects and can be seen in the decorative arts of many cultures. This chapter will explore how patterns and symmetry are fundamental to the designs of quilts, decorative tiles, and in three-dimensional polyhedra.

The mathematics contained in the first section, "The Geometry of Quilts," introduces students to geometric transformations and the mathematics inherent in the basic design of quilt squares. Two different quilt types are included. The first type is one with which we are most familiar—pioneer-type quilts. These are made using polygons and geometric transformations. The second type, the Hawaiian quilt, is unique to the Hawaiian Islands. Squares are folded into fourths or eighths to form fascinating designs that have both reflective and rotational symmetry.

"Semi-Regular Tessellations: Designs and Angles," the third section, invites students to continue their investigations of symmetry and take it a little deeper—exploring geometric transformations or tiling. The applications involved when geometric shapes are used to tile flat surfaces make this topic a truly real-world application of mathematics. In this section, students will investigate regular and semi-regular tessellations and the mathematics involved.

And finally, "Platonic Solids: Designs in Three Dimensions" gives students the opportunity to explore and build polyhedra with a history that goes back to about 350 BCE and the Greek philosopher and mathematician Plato. One of the twentieth century's great artists, M. C. Escher, was fascinated by the Platonic solids and described them in the following way:

> They symbolize man's longing for harmony and order, but at the same time, their perfection awes us with a sense of our own helplessness. Regular polyhedra are not the inventions of the human mind, for they existed long before mankind appeared on the scene. (Lochner, 1971, p. 49)

These four sections focus on real-world applications of mathematics. Recommendations of art, books, and Web sites that illustrate how they relate to history, cultures from around the world, and literature can be found in the Additional Reading segment at the end of the chapter.

THE GEOMETRY OF QUILTS

Teacher's Planning Information

Background Information and Procedures

Quilting activities engage students in projects that apply mathematics to a real-world context. Quilting requires the designers to understand and use a great deal of mathematics skills and concepts—measurement, geometry, fractions, symmetry, design, and transformations. Visualize a quilt as a plane; when a quilt square is moved in this plane, it is called a transformation. Discuss with students the three types of transformations: translations, reflections, and rotations. Explain that in a **translation** (also called a slide), a shape is moved in a given direction without changing its orientation, so it is an exact duplicate of itself.

Mathematical Connections:
Geometry, fractions, symmetry

Other Curricular Connections:
Social studies, art, literature

Concepts:
Students will:

- Examine the symmetry and fractional parts of quilts
- Design their own quilt using 16 squares and speak about the symmetry in their design

Materials Needed:
- Copies of student worksheets
- Glue sticks
- White paper

Translation:

Then explain and give students an example of a **reflection** (also called a mirror image): Every reflection has a mirror line. An object that is reflected appears backwards.

Reflection:

A **rotation** occurs when a shape is turned in a given direction and angle about a fixed point. A shape can be rotated any number of degrees. The following is an example of a 90° rotation.

Rotation:

Let's look at a quilt square and see what happens when it is rotated around a corner.

The original quilt square:

Rotated 90°, 180°, and 270°:

This same quilt square can be made into an entirely different design by reflecting it:

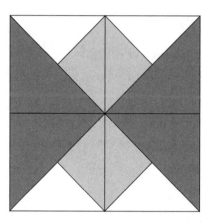

Cross-curricular connections can be made in the language arts and social studies classes. The literature and history of quilting makes cross-cultural connections that help students understand various cultures. In the book, *Hidden in Plain View* (Tobin & Dobard, 2000), a quilt maker, Ozella McDaniels, tells how quilt patterns and colors helped slaves reach safety by using the Underground Railroad. Other books and Web sites listed at the end of the chapter show the integral part that quilting played in pioneer America. These historical events and literature make quilting a truly interdisciplinary journey.

The two mathematics activities in this section related to quilting are "Mathematics and the Snails Trails Quilt Block" and "Designing a Symmetrical Quilt." The first activity has two parts—first, students are asked to calculate what fractional part of the quilt square each shade represents, and second, they are asked to describe the type of symmetry (if any) there is in this square. There are four kinds of symmetry:

H	**M**	**N**	**B**
Symmetry	**Symmetry**	**Symmetry**	**Symmetry**
The object has two mirror lines—one vertical and one horizontal. The right side is a mirror image of the left and the bottom is a mirror image of the top.	The object has one line of symmetry, vertical—the right side is a mirror image of the left side.	The object has no mirror lines (reflective symmetry) but if it is rotated 180°, it appears as the same object. The letters S and Z also have this type of letter symmetry.	The object has one mirror line—the bottom is a mirror image of the top. The letters C and E also have this type of letter symmetry.

The second activity, "Designing a Symmetrical Quilt," provides students with a 16-square template, giving them the opportunity to be mathematically creative as they design their own quilt square. Explain to students that four of these 16 squares are to be arranged to make a 4 × 4 square. This is their *original square* and should be glued in the upper left-hand quadrant of the 8 × 8 quilt grid. Then students are to use transformations (translations, reflections, or rotations) to move their design into the upper right-hand quadrant. The design is to be repeated and transformations used to fill the bottom right and bottom left quadrants. A class quilt can be constructed using student work.

Assessment:

1. Student products—Accuracy of calculations on student worksheets

2. Journal question: "There are four different kinds of letter symmetry—H, M, N, and B. Choose one of these and design a quilt square with that type of symmetry."

Quilts—Selected Answers:

Mathematics and the Snails Trails Quilt Block

1. What fractional part of the square is ?

$$\frac{1}{8} + \frac{1}{8} + \frac{1}{16} + \frac{1}{16} + \frac{1}{32} + \frac{1}{32} + \frac{1}{64} + \frac{1}{64} + \frac{1}{64} + \frac{1}{64} + \frac{32}{64} = \frac{1}{2}$$

What fractional part of the square is ?

$$\frac{1}{8} + \frac{1}{16} + \frac{1}{32} + \frac{1}{64} + \frac{1}{64} + \frac{16}{64} = \frac{1}{4}$$

What fractional part of the square is ?

$$\frac{1}{8} + \frac{1}{16} + \frac{1}{32} + \frac{1}{64} + \frac{1}{64} + \frac{16}{64} = \frac{1}{4}$$

2. There is symmetry in the square. There is **H** symmetry and **S** symmetry.

3. Answers will vary because shapes can be combined.

4. and 5. There are 4 sets of congruent triangles and these triangles are all similar. They are 45°-45°-90° triangles. Also, the squares in the center are congruent. They are each 1/64 of the whole square. The outermost triangles are each 1/8 of the whole square, and as we go into the center, the triangles are 1/6, 1/32, and 1/64 of the area of the whole square.

Mathematics and the Snails Trails Quilt Block

Name _____

Date _____ Class _____

There is a lot of mathematics in this design.

1. If we consider the whole square equal to 1:

   What fractional part of the square is [ ] ? _____

   What fractional part of the square is [ ] ? _____

   What fractional part of the square is [ ] ? _____

2. If there was no shading in this quilt square, would it be symmetrical? _____

   Describe what type of symmetry there would be using letters of the alphabet.

3. Name all the polygons you see in this quilt square. Be as specific as possible.

4. Are there any congruent polygons in this quilt square? If so, name them:

5. Are there any similar polygons in this quilt square? If so, name them:

Designing a Symmetrical Quilt

You will use this grid to design your own quilt. Cut out 16 quilt tiles from the next page. Use them to design your first 4 × 4 square in quadrant #1 (in the upper left of the 16 × 16 quilt pattern block below). Use the remaining quilt tiles to complete your design by rotating, reflecting, or translating the pattern to quadrant #2 (on the upper right). Continue your transformation until you have a complete quilt pattern block.

Quadrant #1   Quadrant #2

Quadrant #3   Quadrant #4

Designing a Symmetrical Quilt: Tiles to Complete the Quilt

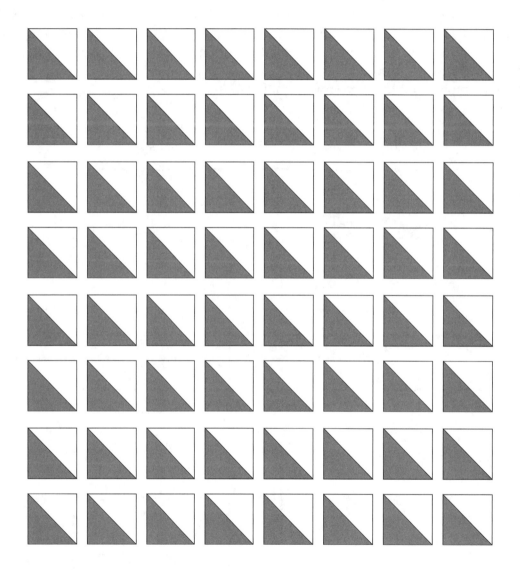

Designing a Symmetrical Quilt: Journal Entry

Describe the following:

(1) How you designed your original 4 × 4 square (the one in quadrant #1).

(2) What transformation you used to replicate it in quadrant #2, then #3, then #4.

(3) What type(s) of symmetry your quilt square exhibits. Explain your answer.

_____

_____

_____

_____

_____

_____

_____

_____

_____

_____

_____

THE HAWAIIAN QUILT SQUARE

Teacher's Planning Information

Background Information and Procedures:

Mathematical Connections:
Spatial visualization, symmetry, problem solving

Other Curricular Connections:
Social studies, art

Concepts:
Students will:

- Paper-fold and design a Hawaiian quilt square
- Apply spatial visualization skills to the design formed from a folded square

Materials Needed:

- Square piece of 8 1/2 x 8 1/2-inch piece of white paper for each student
- Scissors
- Sheet of construction paper sized 10 1/2 x 10 1/2 inches for each student
- Glue or glue sticks

Hawaiian women were taught by missionaries to make quilts, but they found the techniques to be confusing. They could not understand cutting up material to sew the pieces back together again, and the weather did not get cold enough to warrant the use of quilts in the islands.

However, the Hawaiians watched, listened, and learned, and then adapted quilting to their own unique style. The designs the women adapted into their unique Hawaiian quilts were based on the *tapa* designs that they created and placed on their clothing before the foreigners came to the islands.

The quilt designs would eventually be created in a 1/4 or 1/8 design. The Hawaiians were able to take a full piece of material, fold it into their 1/4 or 1/8 design, cut out their pattern, and lay out their quilt. The excess material was then given back to the missionaries for their quilts.

This activity, "The Hawaiian Quilt Square," uses a 1/4 design—when students fold the large square of paper into fourths, the pattern that develops has both reflective and rotational symmetry.

Assessment:

1. Quality of Hawaiian quilt square design

2. Journal question: "Explain how the techniques used by Hawaiian quilters differ from the traditional quilt block squares of our pioneers."

The Hawaiian Quilt Square

Name _____

Date _____ Class _____

Step 1:
Fold a square piece of paper in half; folding from top to bottom (as shown). The opening will be on the bottom.

Step 2:
Without unfolding, fold the paper from left to right (as shown). The openings will be on the bottom and on the right.

Step 3:
Your folded square will be 1/4 the size of the original square. After you draw a design on the square, you will cut it as shown to form your Hawaiian quilt square.

This is an enlarged picture of the folded square shown in Step 3 onto which a sample of a Hawaiian quilt pattern has been drawn.

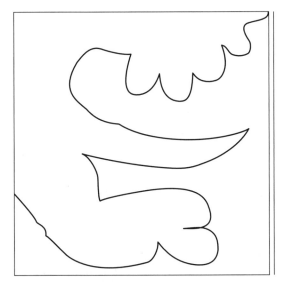

1. Can you predict what the design will look like when the square is unfolded?

2. Describe any symmetry that there might be in the opened square:

Now fold your square and design your own Hawaiian quilt square. When you are finished, glue it onto a square of construction paper that has a 1-inch larger border.

SEMI-REGULAR TESSELLATIONS: DESIGNS AND ANGLES

Teacher's Planning Information

Background Information and Procedures

Geometric tilings or tessellations are an important aspect of both mathematics and art. In addition, because intricate geometric patterns are the basis of the art of many different cultures, these harmonious designs help connect this activity to social studies, as well as art.

Discuss with student that the simplest of tessellations are **regular tessellations** or tessellations that are made up of congruent regular polygons. There are only three regular polygons that tessellate in the Euclidean plane: triangles, quadrilaterals, and hexagons. Here are some examples:

This is a tessellation of triangles: It is named 3.3.3.3.3 because five triangles surround the vertex or point. The five 3s indicate that there are five polygons, each containing three angles.

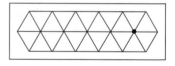

This is a tessellation of squares: It is named 4.4.4.4 because four quadrilaterals surround the vertex or point.

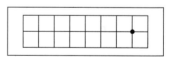

This is a tessellation of hexagons: It is named 6.6.6 because three hexagons surround the vertex or point.

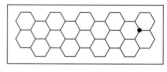

When students understand the definition of regular tessellations, explain that some tessellations are made up of more than one regular polygon. A semi-regular tessellation has two properties: (1) it is formed by regular polygons, and (2) the arrangement of polygons at every vertex point is identical. There are only eight semi-regular tessellations:

Mathematical Connections:
Geometry, fractions, symmetry

Other Curricular Connections:
Social studies, art, literature

Concepts:
Students will:

- Learn how to calculate the number of degrees in the interior angles of regular polygons
- Use their knowledge of interior angles to find the eight semi-regular tessellations

Materials Needed:
- One copy of "Regular Polygons" worksheet (This can be copied onto card stock)
- Scissors
- Paper
- Markers or colored pencils
- Overhead transparency of "To Tessellate or Not to Tessellate?"
- Copy of "To Tessellate or Not to Tessellate?" for each pair of students

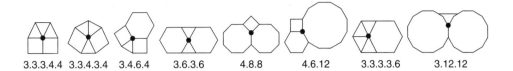

3.3.3.4.4   3.3.4.3.4   3.4.6.4   3.6.3.6   4.8.8   4.6.12   3.3.3.3.6   3.12.12

Table of Semi-Regular Tessellations Pictures Above

	Numerical Code	Geometric Shapes
1	4.4.3.3.3	Two squares and three triangles at each vertex
2	3.3.4.3.4	Two triangles, a square, a triangle, and a square at each vertex. Note: this differs from #4 because of the order or arrangement of polygons.
3	3.4.6.4	A triangle, a square, a hexagon, and another square at each vertex
4	3.6.3.6	A triangle, a hexagon, a triangle, and a hexagon at each vertex
5	4.8.8	A square, and two octagons at each vertex. Note: this is the only semi-regular tessellation that uses octagons.
6	4.6.12	A square, a hexagon, and a dodecagon at each vertex
7	3.3.3.3.6	Four triangles and a hexagon at each vertex
8	3.12.12	A triangle and two dodecagons at each vertex

Please do *not* share the information in the table above with students, as this discovery-type lesson has been designed to allow students to explore, on their own, the combinations of regular polygons that will tile the plane. When a student finds a combination of polygons that will tessellate, tape it to the board and label it with its correct title (e.g., 3.6.3.6). Each student will need a copy of the Regular Polygons worksheet. If the sheet has been duplicated on tag board, students can cut out the shapes and use them as pattern pieces. Students will have difficulty finding the combinations of polygons that will create semi-regular tessellations since not all the regular polygons on the sheet will, in fact, tessellate the plane. Be prepared to use a great deal of paper! When students have discovered at least four semi-regular tessellations, you can enter into the following discussion:

1. Perhaps if we explore why these combinations work mathematically, it will be easier to find the other four semi-regular tessellations.

2. Do you think it might correlate to the sum of the angles at any given vertex?

3. If we draw around any vertex, what geometric shape is formed? How many degrees are there in this shape?

4. So the sum of all of the angles in the interior of this shape must equal how many degrees?

5. Is there a strategy we can use to find how many degrees there are in the angles of the regular polygons we've been using?

Give each student a copy of the worksheet, "To Tessellate or Not to Tessellate?" Use an overhead transparency, and analyze the student examples of semi-regular tessellations. For example, if one of the samples displayed is a 3.6.3.6, the worksheet shows that regular triangles have 60° in each angle and regular hexagons have 120° in each angle. So 3.6.3.6 is equal to 60° + 60° + 120° + 120° or 360°. Students will find, when they analyze the semi-regular tessellations that have been collected, that the angles surrounding any vertex have a sum of 360°. With this new knowledge, students can proceed to find all eight semi-regular tessellations.

Assessment:

1. Semi-regular tessellations designed by students

2. Journal question: "Explain why combinations of polygons that contain pentagons and decagons will not tessellate the plane." [Answers may vary, but the central angles of a regular pentagon are 108° and of a regular decagon are 144°, and combinations of these with any other regular polygons will not produce a sum of 360°.]

Selected Answers:

To Tessellate or Not to Tessellate?

1. There are two fewer triangles than sides.

2. The formula for finding the number of degrees in interior angles of regular polygons is on the table below.

Polygon's Name	Number of Triangles	Total Number of Degrees (# of Triangle × 180°)	Total Number of Angles	Degrees in Each Angle $\dfrac{\text{Total \# of Degrees}}{\text{Total \# of Angles}}$
Triangle	1	180°	3	180°/3 = 60°
Square	2	360°	4	360°/4 = 90°
Pentagon	3	540°	5	540°/5 = 108°
Hexagon	4	720°	6	720°/6 = 120°
Octagon	6	1080°	8	1080°/8 = 135°
Decagon	8	1440°	10	1440°/10 = 144°
Dodecagon	10	1800°	12	1800°/12 = 150°
"N-sided" Polygon	$n - 2$	$180°(n - 2)$	n	$\dfrac{180°(n - 2)}{n}$

Regular Polygons

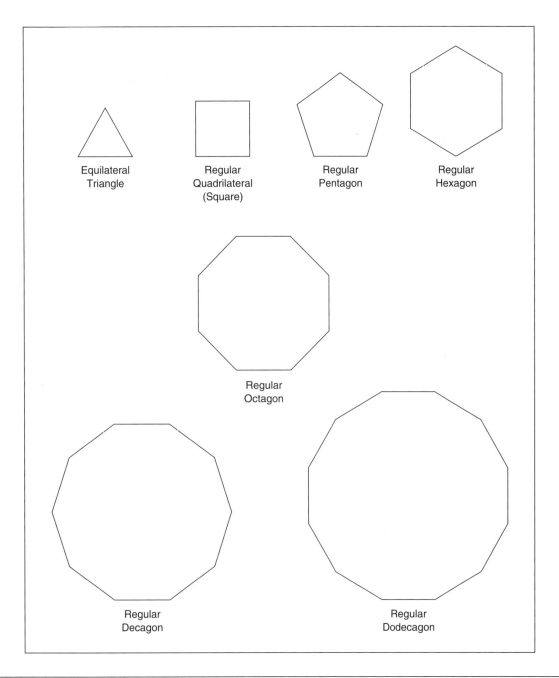

Equilateral Triangle

Regular Quadrilateral (Square)

Regular Pentagon

Regular Hexagon

Regular Octagon

Regular Decagon

Regular Dodecagon

To Tessellate or Not to Tessellate?

Name _____

Date _____ Class _____

Directions: Since we know that the interior angles of any triangle have a sum of 180°, we can use this knowledge to help us problem-solve the number of degrees in each interior angle of any regular polygon. Let's complete this table to help us discover a strategy to find all of the eight semi-regular tessellations!

Polygon's Shape	Polygon's Name	Number of Triangles	Total Number of Degrees (# of Triangles × 180°)	Total Number of Angles	Degrees in Each Angle Total # of Degrees / Total # of Angles
△	Triangle				
□	Square				
⬠	Pentagon				
⬡	Hexagon				
⯃	Octagon				
◯	Decagon				
◯	Dodecagon				
An "N-sided" Polygon					

What pattern develops between the number of sides of the polygon and the number of triangles? Describe it:

PLATONIC SOLIDS: DESIGNS IN THREE DIMENSIONS

Teacher's Planning Information

Background Information and Procedures

These lessons explore solid geometry and regular polyhedra, known as Platonic solids.

Explain to students that regular polyhedra are geometric solids whose faces are all congruent. These polyhedra also have the same number of faces meeting at each vertex. There are only five regular convex polyhedra—they are pictured below.

The ancient Greeks believed the five solids corresponded to the following elements:

Tetrahedron	Fire
Hexahedron (Cube)	Earth
Octahedron	Air
Icosahedron	Water
Dodecahedron	Universe

There are three activities that make up this lesson: (1) The first activity introduces students to the polygons that make up each of the Platonic solids; 2) the second activity supplies students with nets (two-dimensional representations) of each of the polyhedra and encourages them to pick one of the nets, design one face, and reproduce that design on the other faces to from a three-dimensional, symmetric design; and 3) the third activity relates to Euler's polyhedron theorem ($v + f - e = 2$, where v stands for vertices, f stands for faces, and e stands for edges).

Mathematical Connections:
Solid geometry, two-dimensional nets, design symmetry

Other Curricular Connections:
Social studies, art, literature

Concepts:
Students will:

- Learn about Plato's five regular polyhedra
- Use two-dimensional nets to construct the five Platonic solids
- Analyze the shapes and apply Euler's theorem
- Choose one of the Platonic solid nets and create a design on one of its faces, then replicate it on the other faces to create a polyhedron with design symmetry

Materials Needed:
- Student worksheet, "Platonic Solids," for each student
- Nets of Platonic solids for each pair of students
- Scissors
- Colored pencils or markers
- Rulers

Tetrahedron

Hexahedron (Cube)

Octahedron

Icosahedron

Dodecahedron

Assessment:

1. Student products

2. Journal question: "Discuss the Platonic solids. Be sure to explain how many there are, how their names indicate the number of faces, and which polygons they are composed of."

Selected Answers:

Platonic Solids

1. Tetrahedron: Four equilateral triangles

2. Hexahedron (cube): Six squares

3. Octahedron: Eight equilateral triangles

4. Icosahedron: Twenty equilateral triangles

5. Dodecahedron: Twelve regular pentagons

Euler's polyhedron theorem is $v + f - e = 2$, but students may express this formula in a variety of ways. For example, they may express it as $v + f - 2 = e$. Be sure to give students the opportunity to explain how they reasoned out their unique solution.

3-D Explorations (Answers)

Name of Shape	What It Looks Like	Number of Faces	Number of Vertices	Number of Edges
Tetrahedron		4	4	6
Hexahedron (Cube)	Pictures of polyhedra will vary.	6	8	12
Octahedron		8	6	12
Icosahedron		20	12	30
Dodecahedron		12	20	30

Platonic Solids

Name _____

Date _____ Class _____

In 350 BCE, Plato, a Greek philosopher, demonstrated how to construct five special polyhedra that are three-dimensional, solid geometric shapes. He wrote about them in his book *Timaeus*, and the solids became known as the Platonic solids. These are regular polyhedra because each of the faces is a congruent polygon and the same number of faces meet at each vertex. The five polyhedra below are the Platonic solids. Be sure to examine each of the faces and vertices.

| Tetrahedron | Hexahedron (Cube) | Octahedron | Icosahedron | Dodecahedron |

The ancient Greeks believed that each of these solids harmonized to elements in the universe (or the universe itself, in the case of the dodecahedron) as follows:

Tetrahedron = Fire
Hexahedron = Earth
Octahedron = Air
Icosahedron = Water
Dodecahedron = Universe

Describe what polygons and how many of each make up these solids:

1. Tetrahedron _____

2. Hexahedron _____

3. Octahedron _____

4. Icosahedron _____

5. Dodecahedron _____

Platonic Solid Nets

Directions: Cut on the solid lines and fold on the dotted lines. Tuck the tabs inside the polyhedron and use scotch tape to make your Platonic solids. *But before you fold them,* choose your favorite Platonic solid and design one of the sides. Then copy that design onto all of the other faces. Now you can fold and tape your three-dimensional work of art!

Tetrahedron

Hexahedron (Cube)

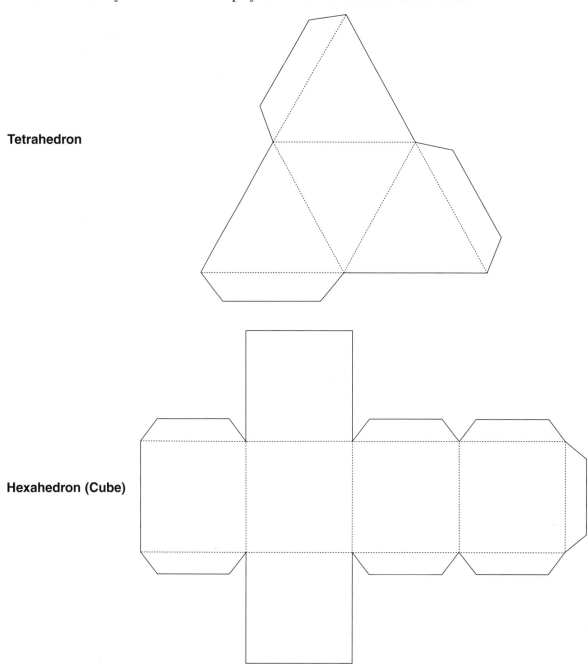

Platonic Solid Nets

Octahedron

Icosahedron

Dodecahedron

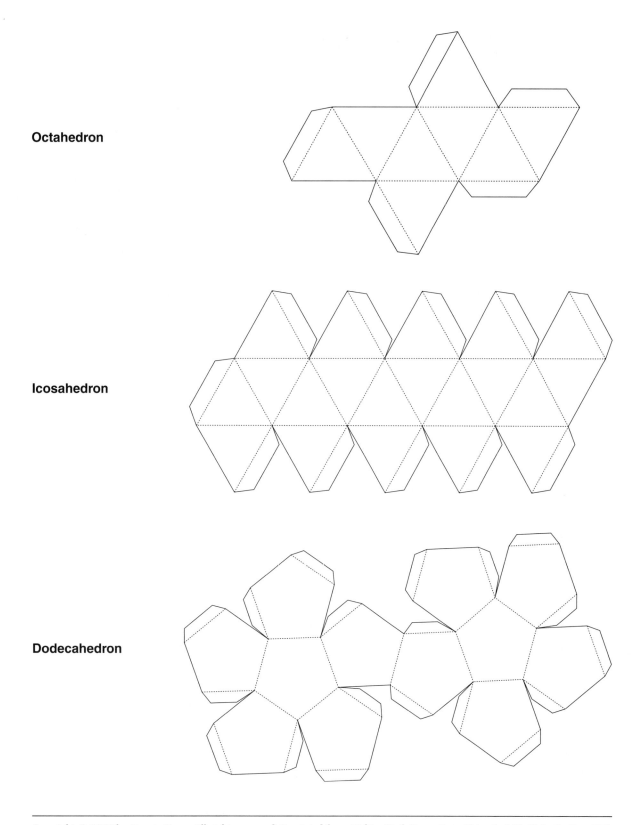

3-D Explorations

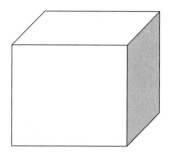

Name _____

Date _____ Class _____

Name of Shape	What It Looks Like	Number of Faces	Number of Vertices	Number of Edges
Tetrahedron				
Hexahedron (Cube)				
Octahedron				
Icosahedron				
Dodecahedron				

Can you find the pattern between the edges, vertices, and faces? Work with your partner to discover this pattern and write it as a formula:

ADDITIONAL READING

Quilts:

Cobb, M. (1995). *The quilt-bloc history of pioneer days: With projects kids can make.* Brookfield, CT: Millbrook Press.

This book contains a brief history of quilts and then, using official quilt-block squares, has projects children can make that incorporate the designs.

Ernst, L. C. (1983). *Sam Johnson and the blue ribbon quilt.* New York: Mulberry.

Sam Johnson finds he enjoys sewing and wants to join his wife's quilting bee. When he is turned down because he is a man, he organizes a rival sewing circle of all men. Both quilting circles race to win the big prize at the State Fair. The border of each of the book's pages is an actual print pattern: Hole in the Barn Door, Variable Star, Rising Sun, Double Wedding Rings, Shoo Fly, Flying Geese, Sailboats, and more.

Hickey, Mary. (1992). *Pioneer storybook quilts.* Bothell, WA: That Patchwork Place.

This book is divided into two sections. The first gives readers the basics of quilt construction. The rest of the book intertwines stories of pioneer America with quilt patterns and the directions for making that quilt. For example, the first story is called "Her Royal Highness, Henrietta the Chicken" and tells the story of Henrietta, a dignified and high-minded breed of chicken with an almost human personality. The quilts that follow the story are called "Chicken Baskets" and "Pioneer Pinwheels."

Hopkinson, D. (2002). *Under the quilt of night.* New York: Atheneum/Anne Schwartz Books.

Paintings and verse-like prose combine to tell the experiences of a young runaway slave as she escapes to Canada via concealed routes and dangerous nighttime treks. The metaphor of a protective quilt of night is combined with the legend that quilts with blue center squares indicated safe houses on the Underground Railroad to tell this story.

Lyons, Mary. (1997). *Stitching stars: The story quilts of Harriet Powers.* New York: Aladdin.

Born an American slave in 1837, Harriet Powers created quilts that are now on display in the Smithsonian. This book tells the story behind the quilts Harriet Powers created.

Polacco, P. (1998). *The keeping quilt.* New York: Simon & Schuster.

When Patricia's great-grandmother came to America from Russia, the only two things she brought were her dress and a babushka. The dress and the babushka soon became part of a quilt along with pieces of clothing from aunts and uncles. This quilt was passed down through the generations and its story is told in this book.

Tobin, J. L., & Dobard, R. (2000). *Hidden in plain view: A secret story of quilts and the Underground Railroad.* New York: Anchor.

When Jacqueline Tobin met quiltmaker Ozella McDaniels, she was told of the Underground Railroad Quilt Code and its place within the history of the Underground Railroad. Each slave quilt, which could be laid out to air without arousing suspicion, gave slaves directions for their escape. Quilt patterns like the wagon wheel, log cabin, and shoo fly signaled slaves how and when to prepare for their journey and certain stitches and knots created maps, showing slaves the way to safety. The stories Ozella told were connected to other forms of hidden communication from history books, codes, and songs.

Tessellations:

Britton, J. (1999). *Symmetry and tessellations: Investigating patterns, grades 5–8.* Palo Alto, CA: Dale Seymour Publications.

This book provides over 30 activities to teach the topics of symmetry, polygons, and tessellations using challenging activities. The book includes 100 blackline masters, a sample set of mirrors, a sheet of tessellating shapes, and dot paper. Grades 5 to 8.

Stephens, P. G. (2001). *Tessellations: The history and making of symmetrical designs.* Glenview, IL: Crystal Productions.

This book provides a step-by-step look at how to create translations, rotations, and reflections. Written with students and teachers in mind, this picture book provides clearly illustrated demonstrations that can be used for independent study or as a teacher resource.

Three-Dimensional Geometry:

Schattschneider, D., & Fetter, A. (1990). *Platonic solids activity book.* Emeryville, CA: Key Curriculum Press.

Activities explore regular and nonregular polyhedra, three-dimensional symmetry, and Euler's theorem.

Sutton, D. (2002). *Platonic & Archimedean solids.* New York: Walker.

Daud Sutton examines both the 8 regular polyhedra (the Platonic solids) and the 10 semi-regular polyhedra (the Archimedean solids) that are the universal building blocks of three-dimensional space, and shows the fascinating relationships between them.

Wenninger, M. J. (1974). *Polyhedron models.* New York: Cambridge University Press.

Easy-to-follow descriptions of how all the known regular polyhedra and some of the "stellated" polyhedra (polyhedra that look like stars) may be constructed. Carefully illustrated with drawings and photographs.

INTERNET WEB SITES

Quilts:

http://www.quilt.com/index.html

> A site designed for quilters that includes a large variety of quilt blocks by type and in alphabetical order. There is also a quilt coloring book, a history of quilting around the world, a list of books relating to quilts and quilting, and computer software that is available to help with the design of quilts.

http://www.learner.org/teacherslab/math/geometry/shape/quilts

> A lesson developed by the Annenberg/CBS Math and Science Project entitled "Shape and Space in Geometry" introduces students to four types of symmetry that can be found in quilt block squares.

http://edsitement.neh.gov/view_lesson_plan.asp?id=241

> A site developed by the National Endowment for the Humanities that contains cultural information about quilts, their historical significance, and various Web sites with background information of interest to teachers.

Tessellations:

http://mathworld.wolfram.com/SemiregularTessellation.html

> Each of the eight semi-regular tessellations is pictured along with links to regular tessellations, demi-regular tessellations, and the Cairo tessellation.

http://library.thinkquest.org/16661/index2.html

> This Web site, known as "Totally Tessellated," tells the history of tessellations, offers a complete discussion of mosaic-type tilings, and describes the tessellations of M. C. Escher. It is a very thorough and user-friendly site for both teacher and student use.

Platonic Solids:

http://www.walter-fendt.de/m14e/platonsolids.htm

> A Java applet that shows each of the Platonic solids and allows the viewer to see the two-dimensional representation in three dimensions as it rotates around a point.

http://www.mathsisfun.com/platonic_solids.html

> The five Platonic solids are illustrated, and next to each, the students have a choice of seeing the net, a model, or a button entitled "spin" that shows the shape spinning. A fact sheet on this page tells how many faces, edges, and sides the shape has, as well as the formulas for calculating its surface area and volume.

http://www.frontiernet.net/~imaging/polyh.html

> This site has three-dimensional representations of the Platonic solids with an interesting twist—it includes a picture of a soccer ball. This shape is an Archimedean solid—a truncated icosahedron. When the corners are chopped off the icosahedron, the shape consists of pentagons and hexagons!

The Stock Market Project 5

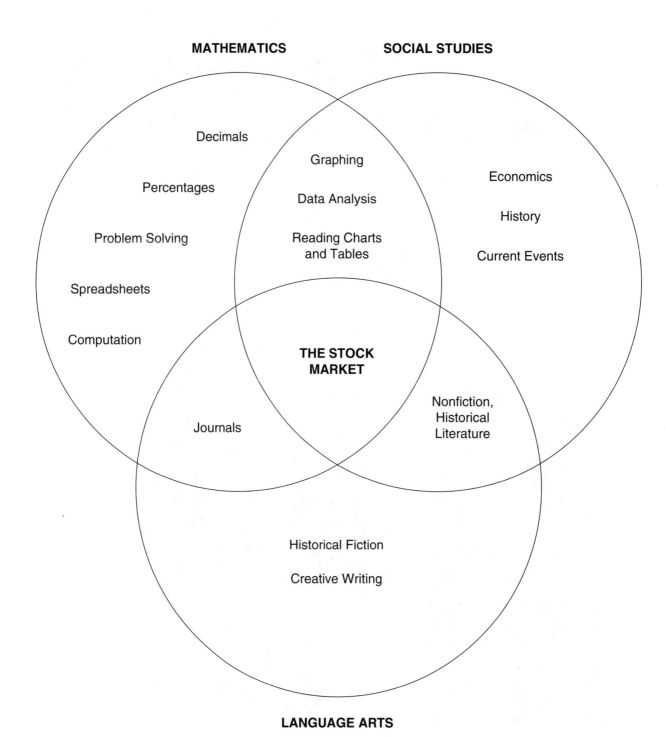

MATHEMATICS

Decimals

Percentages

Problem Solving

Spreadsheets

Computation

SOCIAL STUDIES

Graphing

Data Analysis

Reading Charts
and Tables

Economics

History

Current Events

**THE STOCK
MARKET**

Journals

Nonfiction,
Historical
Literature

Historical Fiction

Creative Writing

LANGUAGE ARTS

The Stock 5
Market Project

INTRODUCTION

The National Council of Teachers of Mathematics (NCTM) Standards maintain that making connections between mathematics and other curricular areas allows students to (1) understand how mathematics relates to their everyday lives, (2) apply mathematical thinking and problem solving to other disciplines, and (3) understand the role mathematics plays in our culture and society. When in the middle grades, students often perceive that school mathematics is unrelated to "real-world" math. By connecting math skills and activities to their applications, teachers can dispel the notion that school mathematics is useless and irrelevant.

One area that supports strong interdisciplinary connections is an extended project introducing students to the stock market. The history of economic growth in the United States shows a country of small, privately owned businesses prior to the 1700s. The Industrial Revolution brought the growth of businesses, and the need for capital encouraged people to open their businesses to new investment. This was the beginning of public corporations, investments, investors, and the stock market. An examination of the interrelationships between economic growth and history makes a rich study in the social studies classroom.

The stock market crash in 1929 and the literature connected with this black day in American history can make exciting connections between history and literature. At the conclusion of this chapter, a list of books and Web sites provides additional resources to enrich this project.

In the mathematics classroom, the stock market project is a wealth of essential middle school studies. Computation, percentages, graphs, accurate record keeping, and integers are just a small part of the mathematics students use to keep track of their "investments" during the course of the project. In addition, spreadsheets can be used to help student keep track of their stocks and supply up-to-date graphs for analysis. Formulas used in these spreadsheets help students translate number patterns into algebraic form.

Many stock market projects involve students for short periods of time—usually 8 to 10 weeks. However, most investors look to the stock market for *long-range investments.* A study of the market shows that over the course of one year, investors can make a profit or lose money, depending on the market. When you extend the time frame to five years of investment, you find that during most five-year periods, investors make money in the stock market! This means that as students invest their "money," they should understand the need for patience and the nature of investing in the stock market. This project has been designed to begin in October and end in May; students keep track of their investments once a week.

Students are placed into groups of four. They are given $10,000 (on paper) to invest and must decide collectively on four different stocks—investing about 25 percent (or $2,500) in each of these stocks. Data collection sheets, such as the "Week-to-Week Stock Market," "Planning to Sell," and "Buying More Stock" sheets help students keep track of their purchases and sales. Finally, at the end of the project, students sell their stocks using the "Final Sale" sheet. This sheet helps them evaluate the following: How much are their groups worth? Have they made a profit? Did they invest wisely? Each phase of the stock market project in this chapter has its own Teacher's Planning Information, similar to those supplied with the other activities and projects. Because some students have difficulty with long-term projects, it is essential that their weekly calculations be monitored closely to prevent small errors from becoming monumental inaccuracies—misconceptions and arithmetic errors can be cleared up quickly if they are controlled weekly.

Observing students during this project is a critical factor of assessment. Each student in the group must be held accountable for the material, especially in such a long-range experience. This is best regulated by careful observation to determine if the following are true:

1. Each student has a viable and important role in the deliberations.

2. Each student has a significant task during calculation.

3. The roles of students rotate so each has an opportunity to assume a particular role.

When setting up the groups, roles can be discussed and the importance of rotation emphasized. The roles of students might be the following:

The Recorder: Enters the data from the newspaper

The Locator: Finds each of the group's stocks closing price in the paper or on the Internet

Two "Computers" or Accountants: Balance the data entries to complete the Week-to-Week Stock Market sheets

Because each job is different and requires an understanding of different skills, it is important to rotate weekly so each student has the opportunity to experience each task.

Some problems may arise as students work together. The following are a few guidelines that may be helpful for the students to know:

1. You are responsible for your own behavior. You must have respect for and consideration of all members of the class. Every group is working hard to keep track of their stocks; they need to be able to concentrate.

2. Your group cannot succeed financially unless you work as a team. You must be willing to help anyone in your group who asks. While working in groups, we are interested in cooperation, not competition.

3. You may not ask the teacher for help unless all members of your group have the same question. Discuss questions within the group before asking for help.

4. Any member of your group may be called on to explain the thinking or reasoning of the group. It is necessary for everyone to understand each part of the project and what the roles involve!

HOW TO READ A STOCK LISTING AND DECIDING ON A STOCK

Teacher's Planning Information

Background Information and Procedures:

Reading the financial section of the newspaper can be very confusing for youngsters, but there is a wealth of information to be found on these pages. The stock market project begins with a short lesson on reading the financial pages and understanding what the column headings mean—"How to Read a Stock Listing."

Place students into groups of four. See if students recognize any of the companies that appear on the New York Stock Exchange or NASDAQ. See if they know anything about any of the companies or if any of them actually owns shares of stock. One of the worksheets included in this lesson, "How to Read a Stock Listing," is a generic example of the columns on the New York Stock Exchange. Give each student a copy of this sheet and go over each of the columns so students become familiar with terms such as dividend and P-E ratio, and what the column headings mean. The newspaper in your community may be slightly different, so you will want to introduce the local stock listing to the students so they can become familiar with what information is supplied in the local paper. Additional worksheets that will help students better understanding the financial pages are "Deciding on a Stock" and "The Dynamics of a Stock." Both of these sheets use imaginary companies so that the worksheets do not become out of date as stock prices change. Work through these sheets with students so that they understand how to read the financial pages and are familiar with the format of the financial data.

Once students understand the financial pages, give students time to discuss, in their groups, eight different stocks in which they might be interested in investing. Each person in the group is to research two of these stocks for a

Mathematical Connections:
Reading data from a table, computation, integers

Other Curricular Connections:
Economics, accounting, technology

Concepts:
Students will:

- Learn to read information from the financial pages in a newspaper
- Analyze numerical information
- Design a broken-line graph to keep track of the closing prices of stocks

Materials Needed:
- A copy of the worksheet "How to Read a Stock Listing" for each group
- A copy of "Keeping Track of a Stock" for each member of the group
- Calculators

period of two weeks. Have them keep track of the closing price each day, graph its ups and downs, calculate how many shares they can purchase with their share of the money, and interview adults to help them make their decisions. If computers are available, this data can be collected and entered on a spreadsheet and graphs can be made using this technology. When the necessary data has been collected, each student will have important financial knowledge to contribute to his or her group.

Now it is time for each group to decide on four stocks they will invest in. The group is given $10,000 to invest equally in four different stocks—about 25% should be invested in each stock. The "Our First Week: Buying Our Four Stocks" sheet is used for this initial investment of funds.

Each phase of the stock market project has an explanation page similar to those supplied with the other interdisciplinary experiences.

Assessment:

1. Student worksheets—"Keeping Track of a Stock"

2. Journal question: "Explain how you chose your two stocks to research and what expert advice you received to help you and your group make your final decisions."

How to Read a Stock Listing—Selected Answers:

1. The column labeled "Close" because that is the price at the end of the day when the stock market closed.

2. No. The Net Change column reflects the change in price from the day before, which may not give the investor needed information. For example, suppose the net change on a stock that is selling for $102.00 is +2.00. That seems a substantial increase but it is an increase of only 2%. Suppose the week before, the stock dropped from a price of $148.00 to $100.00—the stock registered a loss of about 33%! The increase of $2.00 is certainly not enough to make investment in this company less worrisome!

How to Read a Stock Listing and Deciding on a Stock—Selected Answers:

How to Read a Stock Listing

1. The column called "Close" records the closing price of the stock that day.

2. The "Net Change" column tells what the change was from the day before; it does not give any information about the long-term performance of the stock.

The Dynamics of a Stock

1.

    (a) Stock D had the largest range in price. It could mean that the company is unstable or has had major problems. Since it is still selling for the lowest price it's been all year, *bottom feeders* might encourage investors to buy the stock in hopes that it will go back up. However, more conservative investors might stay away from it to see what happens!

    (b) Stock C had the smallest range in price. It could mean that the company is very stable. But aggressive investors might also say that there is not a lot of money to be made with the company!

2. Stock D had an approximate loss of 134%.

3.

    (a) Stock A: 92 shares of stock cost $2,493.20.
    (b) Stock B: 42 shares of stock cost $2,478.00.
    (c) Stock C: 99 shares of stock cost $2,499.75.
    (d) Stock D: 299 shares of stock cost $2,496.65.
    (e) Stock E: 40 shares of stock cost $2,460.00.

How to Read a Stock Listing

Name _____

Date _____ Class _____

Our very unpredictable stock market has been of great interest to many people. But if you're a beginner, it pays to learn the language first. Let's look at a small portion of a stock page and "decipher the codes." The stock abbreviations in the table do not represent real companies.

These prices show the range of the stock's prices over the past 365 days. You can compare them to other stocks in the same industry.

This is the symbol for the stock. It may not be the same in all newspapers.

The stock's annual/share cash return. Most dividends are distributed quarterly, so this amount must be divided by 4 to find the actual amount.

The price-to-earning ratio is the price of the stock divided by the company's earnings. If this number is high, the stock is overpriced.

The total number of shares traded (measured in 100s). Therefore the number listed must be multiplied by 100.

52-Week		Stock	Div	Yld	P-E	Vol Hds	High	Low	Close	Net Chg
High	Low									
17.45	7.00	AAR	.10	1.1	15	847	8.99	8.72	8.93	−.02
18.95	6.10	ABB	...	...	...	112	6.88	6.80	6.87	−.08
38.20	24.96	ABM	.66	2.4	14	364	27.15	26.54	27.15	+.71
26.06	14.30	ABN	.77	5.2	3	4838	14.99	14.65	14.89	+.05
25.90	21.69	ABR	1.88	7.4	...	353	25.59	25.47	25.52	+.02
25.65	20.50	ACE	1.78	7.1	...	468	25.00	24.90	24.97	−.03
28.50	22.00	ACT	2.22	8.9	...	51	26.30	25.00	25.00	−.50
43.94	18.10	ACS	.52	1.3	19	24495	38.99	37.35	38.60	+1.52
50.00	18.75	ADT	...	...	9	6307	36.25	32.00	33.31	−2.90

The high and low represent the range in which the stock traded throughout the day. The close is the price at the last trade of the day (4 PM Eastern Time). The closing price will be used as the cost of the stock in this project.

The net change is the difference between the last trade and the previous day's closing price. *It does not necessarily indicate a trend. It reflects the difference between only two days of trading!*

1. When you are researching to choose a stock, which column(s) do you think will be the most helpful? Why?

2. Will your group be interested in a stock that has a large dividend or one that has a strong growth pattern? Explain your answer.

3. Why will the "Net Change" column be of little assistance when you are choosing stocks? Explain.

4. Which column will your group use when deciding the cost of the stock each week?

The Dynamics of a Stock and Deciding on a Stock

Name _____

Date _____ Class _____

What is the stock market and why do people invest their money in it? The stock market is a group of companies that sell shares to the public. If you buy a share of stock in McDonalds, you own a piece of that company! How do you know what company to invest your money in? We can learn more about the financial health of a company by understanding the information found on the financial pages of a newspaper.

On the next page is a table of stock prices for five imaginary companies. Not all of the columns may look exactly like the ones in your local paper, but they should be fairly similar.

The first column (52-Week High/Low Stock Prices) is the highest price and the lowest price this stock has sold for in the past 52 weeks (the past year).

The second column is the name of the company. Sometimes the newspaper has the name in an abbreviated form and it may be hard to understand the abbreviation. You can use the Internet to help you better understand these abbreviations.

The third column is the number of shares of stock that were sold the previous day (3565 means 356,500).

The fourth column is the highest price anyone paid for the stock on this day, the fifth column is the lowest price, and the sixth column indicates what the stock was selling for when the market closed at 4:00 PM Eastern Time.

The Net Change column is not how much the stock changed during the day but how much it has changed from the day before. If the last column shows +0.25, the stock cost $.25 more today than when it closed yesterday. Use the table on the next page to help you better understand financial information that will help you buy and sell stocks successfully— remember, the goal of your group will be to earn the most money you can!

Use the information on this table to help you answer these questions:

52-Week High/ Low (365 Days)	Stock	Sales in Hundreds	High	Low	Close	Net Change (from previous day)
31.12/22.75	Stock A	7837	27.25	27.10	27.10	+.38
61.54/50.79	Stock B	4646	59.36	58.75	59	+.05
29.33/25.05	Stock C	2067	26.00	25.65	25.25	−.40
32.75/8.25	Stock D	1374	8.50	8.35	8.35	+.10
62.40/41	Stock E	83	62.15	58.72	61.50	—

1. Use the 52-week high/low figures:

    (a) Which stock had the largest range in price? _____ What do you think this might mean?

    (b) Which stock had the smallest range in price? _____ What do you think this might mean?

2. What percentage of loss is shown by Stock D in the past year?

3. Based on the closing prices of these five stocks, how many shares of each could your group purchase for $2,500? (Remember that you cannot buy a fractional part of a stock.)

    (a) Stock A _____

    (b) Stock B _____

    (c) Stock C _____

    (d) Stock D _____

    (e) Stock E _____

Keeping Track of a Stock

Name _____

Date _____ Class _____

Name of stock: _____

My reasons for choosing this stock are: _____

Keeping Track of a Stock Graph

(vertical axis) **Cost of Closing Stock**

(horizontal axis) **Days**

As a result of my research, I will/will not recommend this stock to my group. (Explain which you will do and why.)

Keeping Track of a Stock 2

Name _____

Date _____ Class _____

Name of stock: _____

My reasons for choosing this stock are: _____

Keeping Track of a Stock Graph

Cost of Closing Stock

Days

As a result of my research, I will/will not recommend this stock to my group. (Explain which you will do and why.)

FIRST WEEK TO BUY STOCK

Teacher's Planning Information

Background Information and Procedures:

This is the first meeting of the stock groups. They will need to have consensus about the four stocks that they will be purchasing. It is important that the group (as a whole) agree on the stocks. Each person does not own one stock—the members of the group own four stocks.

Although the groups will be investing approximately $2,500 on each stock, they will need to problem-solve the number of shares they can purchase. Sometimes it is confusing to students that the same amount of money will purchase vastly different amounts of stock—depending on the cost of one share!

Facilitate and assist the groups when questions arise. It is a good idea to allow the groups to solve their own problems. Remember, don't get involved unless everyone in the group has the same problem. Students should be encouraged to solve problems within their groups before turning to you.

Students can obtain stock prices and financial information from newspapers or, if computers are available, on http://biz.yahoo.com/r/. This is only one site that might be used. It allows students to type in the full name of a company and receive the stock abbreviation, closing prices from the day before, and data about the stock over a period of time.

Each group will need four copies of the graph "Closing Stock Prices." The group must decide who will be responsible for maintaining each of the graphs—each member of the group should accept responsibility for graphing the closing price of one the stocks each week. This first week, students must label the axes and plot the closing price of each stock for Week 1. There will be only one dot for the first week but, as the students continue to keep track of the stock, a trend can be determined by the direction of the graph.

Mathematical Connections:
Decimals, percentages, computation, problem solving, reading information from tables, graphing

Other Curricular Connections:
Economics, history, technology

Concepts:
Students will:

- Confirm the stock purchases for their groups
- Determine the number of shares they can purchase of a particular stock at a cost of $2,500
- Calculate the cost of their purchases
- Balance their group bank accounts

Materials Needed:
- Copy of "First Week to Buy Stock" sheet for each group (This sheet is used for this first lesson only.)
- Four copies of the graph "Closing Stock Prices" for each group
- Copy of financial section of newspaper or access to Internet financial information
- File folder for each stock group
- Calculators

Give each group a file folder and indicate where the folders will be stored. At the end of the lesson, have the students place the data collection sheets in the same folder as the graphs of the stocks.

Assessment:

1. Completion of record of first purchases and beginning graph

2. Journal question: "Pretend your group is interested in purchasing a stock that closed at $23.11. What is the maximum number of shares of this stock that can be purchased for $2,500? Explain how you solved this problem." [Answer: 108 shares]

First Week to Buy Stock

Group members: _____

_____

_____

Date of purchase: _____ Date on newspaper or Web page: _____

Use this sheet for your initial stock purchase. *It is the only time you will use this worksheet.* Be sure to balance your group's bank account—you must spend as much of the money as you can. You cannot have more in "D. Money still in the bank" than the cost of one share of any of the stocks!

Name of Stock	Abbreviation for Stock	Number of Cost per Share	Total Shares Purchased	This Cost Is Cost for This Stock	What Percent of $10,000?

Total cost of today's purchases: _____

Use this section to balance your group's bank account. By doing this, you will have a current record of (1) the amount of money you have invested in stocks, and (2) the amount of money you have not spent (money in the bank).

Balancing the Bank

    A. We started with $ _____10,000.00_____

    B. Amount of today's purchases $ _____

    C. Next week we will start out with (A – B) $ _____

    D. Money still in the bank $ _____

Closing Stock Prices

Name _____

Graphic record of _____ (name of stock)

Closing Stock Prices Graph

Closing Cost of Stock

Date

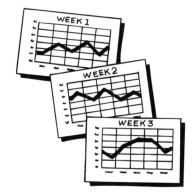

WEEK-TO-WEEK STOCK MARKET

Teacher's Planning Information

Background Information and Procedures:

Allow students time to get their stock portfolios (file folders), a copy of the data collection sheet ("Week-to-Week Stock Market"), and a copy of the financial pages. Be sure that groups have rotated jobs or roles.

At this point, your role is facilitator. If a group is really at a loss and no one in the group seems to be able to solve the problem, work with them to resolve the problem. Otherwise, roam around the room, observe the groups' interactions, and note their progress (or lack of progress).

It is best to check the data sheets as often as possible. If time allows, check each group's sheet and initial it as correct.

Remember, this is the sheet that students will use every week (unless they are selling or buying a new stock.) It is recommended that they keep track of a stock for at least four weeks and that they only be allowed to sell one stock and wait a week before they replace it with a buy.

When students have found the closing costs of each of their stocks and obtained the costs from the previous week, they enter the data on the current sheet, complete their computations, and graph the new dot (price) on their graph.

Assessment:

1. Correct computation on data collection worksheet
2. Journal question: "Explain how your group determined if there was a profit or loss this week. Also, what role did you play in collecting, recording, and calculating profit or loss?"

Mathematical Connections:
Decimals, percentages, integers, computation, problem solving, reading information from a table

Other Curricular Connections:
Economics, accounting, technology

Concepts:
Students will:

- Record the closing price of each of their stocks from the previous week's sheet and find the closing price of their stocks in the newspaper for the current week
- Determine if the difference constitutes a gain (+) or a loss (−)
- Calculate the total amount of profit or loss for each stock
- Compute if their group has made a profit or a loss for the week by finding the sum of the last column
- Balance the bank by adding (a profit) or subtracting (a loss) from the previous week's value
- Maintain the graph of stock prices from week to week

Materials Needed:
- A copy of the financial section of a local paper or access to an Internet financial site
- A copy of the "Week-to-Week Stock Market" sheet for each group
- Calculators

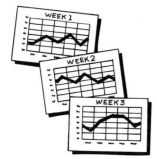

Week-to-Week Stock Market Sheet

Group members: _____

_____

_____

_____

Week #: _____ Date on newspaper or Web page: _____

Use this sheet when your group is keeping track of stocks. Remember, you cannot buy or sell stocks using this sheet. You will also balance your bank account by filling out the bottom section.

Week-to-Week Stock Data Table

Abbreviation for Stock	Number of Shares Owned	Closing Cost of Stock in Last Week's Paper	Closing Cost of Stock in Today's Paper	+ or − How Much?	Profit (+) or Loss (−) × Number of Shares Owned
TOTAL PROFIT OR LOSS THIS WEEK					

Use this section of the sheet to balance your group's bank account. By doing this, you will have a current record of the value of your stock group. *Be sure to keep your graph of each stock up-to-date!*

Balancing the Bank

    A. Last week our stocks were worth (see last week) $ _____

    B. Profit or loss this week $ _____

    C. This week our stocks are worth (A + B or A − B) $ _____

SELL WEEK

Teacher's Planning Information

Background Information and Procedures:

If a group of students has received permission to sell a stock, they will use the "Planning to Sell" sheet instead of the "Week-to-Week Stock Market" sheet. They must sell it early in the data collection process since selling stock is time consuming and cannot be rushed. There are two different processes in this transaction: (1) keeping track of the profit or loss for the stocks the group will keep, and (2) finding the closing price for the stock to be sold and selling all shares at this price.

The amounts are separated in the stock sheet so that the students will not be confused by the transaction. For example: If a group sells $2,300 worth of stock and has $8,000 remaining in investments, their total worth is $10,300. But, the stock they still own is only worth $8,000! Students will often buy $2,300 worth of stock and consider their total worth as $10,300 + $2,300 instead of $8,000 + $2,300. In other words, they count the money both as money *and* as stock! When they purchase stock the following week, they will have $2,300 to buy a new stock and $8,000 in the portfolio that they still own!

It is not wise to allow students to buy and sell during the same week because they tend to work very quickly and are prone to error. By waiting a week, they can think about their investments, research a new stock, and buy stock the following week using the "Buying More Stock" sheet.

The student responsible for the "Closing Stock Prices" graph should indicate on that graph that the stock was sold and the date. Next

Mathematical Connections: Decimals, computation, integers, problem solving

Other Curricular Connections: Current events, economics, technology

Concepts:
Students will:

- Using the "Planning to Sell" sheet, record the closing price of the three stocks they plan to keep from the previous week's sheet and find the closing prices of these stocks in the newspaper for the current week
- Determine if the value of these three stocks has gone up or down and record this as a positive (+) or negative (−) number
- Determine the price of the to-sell stock and enter the necessary information on the sheet
- Find the profit or loss for the stocks remaining in their portfolio and enter that in "B" of the "Balancing the Bank" section
- Calculate the total money they received from the sale of their stock and enter that in "C" of the "Balancing the Bank" section of the sheet

Materials Needed:
- A copy of the financial section of the paper for each group or access to the Internet
- A "Planning to Sell" worksheet for the group that has permission to sell one share of stock
- "Week-to-Week Stock Market" sheets for the other groups
- Calculators

week, when the group buys a new stock, this member will be responsible for keeping track of the new stock.

Assessment:

1. Observation of student groups and correct computation on worksheets

2. Journal question: "Why did your group decide to sell the stock that it did? Did you follow the rule 'Buy low and sell high' ? Why or why not?"

Planning to Sell

Group members: _____

_____

_____

Week #: _____ Date on newspaper or Web page: _____

Use this sheet when your group is planning to sell one of your stocks. First sell the stock and enter the information in the correct place. Then keep track of the three stocks you are planning to keep.

Stocks we will be keeping:

Abbreviation for Stock	Number of Shares Owned	Closing Cost of Stock in Last Week's Paper	Closing Cost of Stock in Today's Paper	+ or − (How Much?)	Profit (+) or Loss (−) × Number of Shares

Profit or loss for the stocks you still own: _____

Stock we will be selling:

Name of Stock We Are Selling	Abbreviation for Stock	Today's Closing Cost per Share	Number of Shares We Are Selling	Total Value of This Stock Sale

Balancing the Bank

A. Money we received from the stock sold today $ _____

B. Last week our stocks were worth $ _____

C. Profit or loss (+ or −) from the three stocks we still own $ _____

D. The stocks we still own are worth (B + C or B − C) $ _____

BUYING MORE STOCK

Teacher's Planning Information

Background Information and Procedures:

Mathematical Connections:
Decimals, computation, integers, problem solving

Other Curricular Connections:
Economics, accounting, technology

Concepts:
Students will:

- Using the "Buying More Stock" sheet, record the closing price of the three stocks the group did not sell the previous week and find the closing prices of these stocks in the newspaper for the current week
- Determine if the value of these three stocks has gone up or down and record this as a positive (+) or negative (–) number
- Determine the price of the stock they wish to buy and enter the necessary information in that part of the "Buying More Stock" sheet
- Calculate the total cost of their new stock and enter that in "B" of the "Balancing the Bank" section of the sheet
- Find the profit or loss for the stocks remaining in their portfolio and enter that in "A" of the "Balancing the Bank" section of the sheet (This can be found in "D" of last week's "Balancing the Bank" section.)
- Find the value of all of their stock (including new purchase) and record their net worth

Materials Needed:
- A copy of the financial section of the paper for each group or access to the Internet
- A "Buying More Stock" worksheet for the group that is replacing the stock that was sold the previous week
- "Week-to-Week Stock Market" sheets for the other groups
- Calculators

Students must agree on and buy a stock early in the data collection process. This is time consuming and cannot be rushed. The two most important processes in this transaction are (1) to keep track of the profit or loss for the stocks the group has not sold, and (2) to find the closing price for the stock to be bought during the current week with the money the group received from the previous week's sale.

The amount of money the group has to invest in a new stock can be found in "A" of the "Balancing the Bank" section of the week the old stock was sold. This figure should represent only the amount of money received from the sale of the one stock. The amount of money they use to purchase shares in the new stock must be equal to the amount of money they received from the sale the previous week. If some funds are not used, the group must keep a record of it so it can be added to their total value on the last week.

A new "Closing Stock Prices" graph must be started for the new stock purchase.

Assessment:

1. Observation of student groups and correct computation on worksheets

2. Journal question: "What research did your group use to help it decide to buy the stock that it did?"

Buying More Stock

Group members: _____

_____

Week #: _____ Date on newspaper or Web page: _____

Use this sheet when your group is planning to replace the one stock that you sold. Then keep track of the three stocks you did not sell in the usual way.

Stocks we will be selling:

Abbreviation for Stock	Number of Shares Owned	Closing Cost of Stock in Last Week's Paper	Closing Cost of Stock in Today's Paper	+ or − (How Much?)	Profit (+) or Loss (−) × Number of Shares

Profit or loss for the stocks you still own: _____

Stock we will be buying:

Name of Stock We Are Buying	Abbreviation of Stock	Today's Closing Cost per Share	Number of Shares We Are Buying	Total Value of This Stock Buy*

*This cannot exceed the amount of your sale last week (Can be found in last week's *Balancing the Bank* "A")

Balancing the Bank

A. Last week our stocks were worth (Look at "D" of last week's worksheet) $ _____

B. Total cost of the stock bought today $ _____

C. Profit or loss (+ or −) from the three stocks we did not sell $ _____

D. This week our group is worth [(A+B) +/−C)] $ _____

OUR FINAL SELL WEEK

Teacher's Planning Information

Background Information and Procedures:

At this point, students will be selling all of their stocks to determine the total value of their group at the end of the project. For this reason, they are not concerned with the value of the stock in last week's paper but only with the closing costs for the current week.

For example, if the total value of their sale is $15,200, then the group made a profit of $5,200 (since they began the project with $10,000.) They can compute their percentage of profit with the following formula:

$$\% \text{ of profit} = \frac{\text{difference } (\$5,200)}{\text{original money } (\$10,000)} = 0.52 = 52\%$$

This group did very well in their adventures in the stock market!

Assessment:

1. If students have been required to maintain computer records of their weekly transactions or make corrections on a weekly or monthly basis, then the computations on this final sheet can be compared with those frequent checks.

2. Journal question: "List the strengths and weaknesses of your group during this long-term data collection project. How do you think your group could have increased its profit or decreased its loss?"

Mathematical Connections:
Decimals, computation, integers, problem solving

Other Curricular Connections:
Economics, accounting, technology

Concepts:
Students will:

- Find the closing prices of their stock in the newspaper (or on the Internet) for the current week and record them
- Calculate the value of their stock at the closing price
- Balance the bank by adding the money received from the sale of their stock to any money that remains unspent (in the bank)
- Determine the total value of their group at the end of the project
- Calculate the percentage of profit (or loss) for their group

Materials Needed:
- A copy of the financial section of the newspaper for each group or access to the Internet
- A copy of "The Final Sale" worksheet for each group
- Calculators

The Final Sale

Group members: _____

_____

_____

Week #: _____ Date on newspaper or Web page: _____

Your group will use this sheet to sell all of your currently owned stocks and find your final value. Be sure to add any money that is left unspent (in the bank).

Name of Stock	Abbreviation for Stock	Closing Cost per Share	Number of Shares to Sell	Total Money for Selling This Stock

Total receipt for today's final sale: _____

Balancing the Bank

    A. Money received from sale of stock $ _____

    B. Money in the bank $ _____

    C. At the end of the project we have $ _____

Now you can calculate your percentage of profit by using this simple formula:

$$\frac{\text{amount of profit}}{\$10,000} \times 100$$

Our percentage of profit = _____

If your group lost money, then you will have a percentage of loss. This can be calculated using the same formula.

ADDITIONAL READING

Bateman, K. R. (2001). *The young investor: Projects and activities for making your money grow*. Chicago: Chicago Review Press.

> This book explains the language of business and the skill of investing. Dozens of activities teach how to balance a checkbook, read stock tables, and know what people are talking about when they mention inflation, recession, and the Federal Reserve Board.

Caes, C., & Caeser, C. (2000). *Young zillionaire's guide to the stock market*. New York: Rosen.

> Written for students in Grades 5 to 8, this book provides basic information on the stock market including stock splits, bear and bull markets, and more. The companies used as examples are familiar to students (e.g., PepsiCo, McDonald's, and IBM).

Fisher, C. P. (1993). *The stock market explained for young investors*. Woodside, CA: Business Classics.

> A comprehensive look at the stock exchange, stocks, stock ownership, investments, and stock options for young investors.

Gow, M. (2003). *Stock market crash of 1929: Dawn of the Great Depression*. Berkeley Heights, NJ: Enslow.

> This nonfiction book describes the 1929 stock market crash and the despair that followed through firsthand accounts and quotes. The author also examines subsequent economic crises up to the present day.

McGowen, E. N., & Dumas, N. L. (2002). *Stock market smart*. Minneapolis, MN: Lerner.

> Written for students in Grades 5 to 8, this book takes a complex subject and simplifies it! The book includes chapters on "Setting Up a Portfolio," "Buying and Selling Stocks," and a section called "For More Information" that lists relevant books, a game, and Web sites.

Sharmat, M. (1994). *Hello . . . this is my father speaking*. New York: HarperCollins.

> Jeff Whitty is embarrassed that his father cleans offices for a living, so he invests in the stock market. His desire is to make enough money to allow his father to quit his job.

INTERNET WEB SITES

http://www.smgww.org

> The Stock Market Game gives students the chance to invest a hypothetical $100,000 in a real-time portfolio.

http://library.thinkquest.org/3096

> This Web site is designed *by* kids *for* kids. It examines stocks, bonds, mutual funds, and the like. It teaches the principles of saving and investing.

http://lessonplancentral.com/lessons/Economics/Stock_Market

A collection of lesson plans that help students learn how the stock market works, how to choose stocks, and how to examine market trends.

http://webtech.kennesaw.edu/jcheek3/stock_market.htm

A Web site of stock market resources for kids including games, simulations, and a list of sites that explain stocks and the stock market.

Math and Literature 6

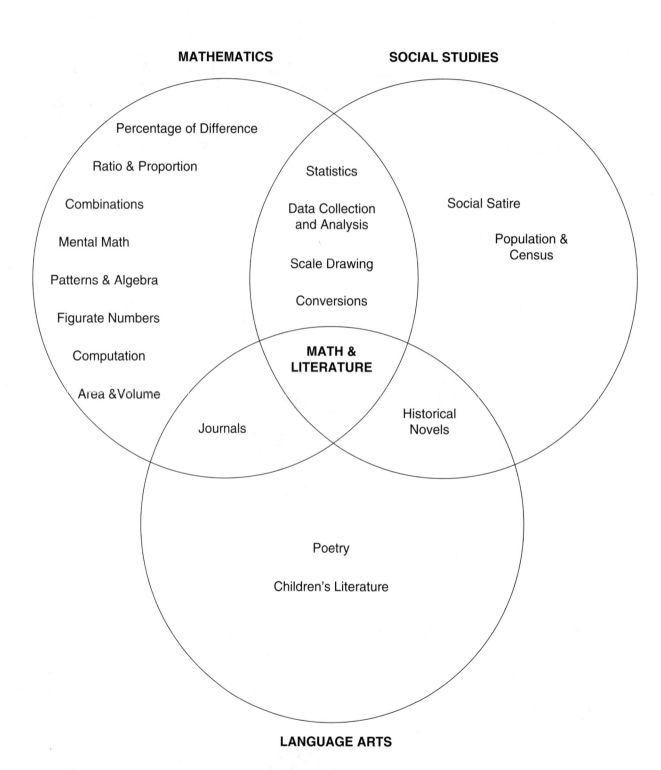

MATHEMATICS

SOCIAL STUDIES

Percentage of Difference

Ratio & Proportion

Combinations

Mental Math

Patterns & Algebra

Figurate Numbers

Computation

Area & Volume

Statistics

Data Collection
and Analysis

Scale Drawing

Conversions

Social Satire

Population &
Census

**MATH &
LITERATURE**

Journals

Historical
Novels

Poetry

Children's Literature

LANGUAGE ARTS

Math and Literature 6

The true spirit of delight, the exaltation, the sense of being more than Man, which is the touchstone of the highest excellence, is to be found in mathematics as surely as in poetry.

—Bertrand Russell (1892–1970)

INTRODUCTION

The activities in this chapter are divided into three sections: (1) Looking for Math in Poetry, (2) Traveling to Lilliput: How Small Were the Lilliputians?, and (3) A Million Is a Very Big Number.

"Looking for Math in Poetry" includes a collection of three poems written by Shel Silverstein. The first poem, "Keepin' Count," tells the story of a little boy who is trying to count the flies in a jar and not having much success. This math activity tackles the problem scientists have of "counting" populations that are either too big or too mobile to count in a traditional manner. By using a capture–recapture simulation called "Capture–Recapture: How Many Beans?" students see how ratio and proportion can be used to estimate the size of populations.

The second poem, "Ice Cream Stop," tells the tale of a circus train of animals that stops at an ice cream stand that has 52 flavors of ice cream. Students, in the activity "Flavors of Ice Cream," are asked to calculate how many combinations of two-flavor, double-scoop cones can be made from first small numbers of flavors and working up to 52 different flavors.

The last poem, "Overdues," tells the tale of a man who has a library book that is 42 years overdue! In the activity, "Overdue Book Fines," simple computation and conversions reveal the cost of such forgetfulness.

"Traveling to Lilliput: How Little Were the Lilliputians?" challenges students to answer the questions, "If a person is only 6 inches tall, how big do you think his head would be? His arms? His legs?" Then, by using ratio and proportion, data collection, and scale drawing, students draw a picture of a Lilliputian.

"A Million Is a Very Big Number" uses hands-on activities to help students *visualize* the size of millions and billions. John Paulos, in his book *Innumeracy* (1988), bemoans our ignorance of large numbers. How much of a difference is there between a million and a billion? How long ago was a million seconds, a billion seconds, or a trillion seconds? Ask your students to solve these problems—you might be surprised by their answers. There are three problems to help students get a handle on big numbers.

The Toothpaste Millionaire, by Jean Merrill, serves as the setting for the first "big number" activity—"Spending $1,000,000." Students calculate how long it will take Rufus Mayflower (the hero) to spend a million dollars. Then, by using computers and spreadsheets, students can calculate how long it would take to spend 1,000 times as much money—a billion dollars.

In David Schwartz's book, *If You Made a Million*, a little girl earns a penny, a nickel (5 pennies), a dime (10 pennies), and so on until she earns a million dollars. When she has earned 1 million pennies, how big a box will they fit in? Students build an open-top box and use it to estimate and solve the problem, "How Big a Box Do We Need for 1,000,000 Pennies?"

And finally, in *How Much Is a Million* by David Schwartz, students see a sky filled with stars and are asked to estimate how many pages it would take to picture one million stars. Our own version of "A Million Stars" asks students to problem-solve how many pages of stars like their sample it would take to show one million stars—how much would that amount of paper weigh? Would there be enough sheets to wallpaper their classroom?

LOOKING FOR MATH IN POETRY: CAPTURE-RECAPTURE: HOW MANY BEANS?

Teacher's Planning Information

Background Information and Procedures:

Begin by reading Shel Silverstein's poem, "Keepin' Count." This poem can be found in his book, *Falling Up.* The poem tells the story of a professor who offers a young child a prize if he can accurately count all of the flies in a jar. After counting more than 3 million, a new fly is born and he has to start all over again. Ask students, "Do you think that it is possible to count all the flies in a jar? Why or why not? How do we 'count' populations that are either too big, move around too much, or cannot be seen? Mathematicians have developed a data collection technique that helps us estimate populations that are like this."

Discuss how naturalists and environmentalists use a data collection technique called "capture-recapture." Capture-recapture has traditionally been employed in biometrics (the statistical study of biological events). particularly in the estimation of animal populations. Recently, the technique has been adopted to study human populations because using traditional census techniques might result in undercounting the population. While it is sometimes criticized as being only an estimate, it is effective when traditional counting techniques are impossible or are very often inaccurate.

It does have some drawbacks, however. In the case of estimating animal populations, if it is not done properly and populations are overestimated or underestimated, decisions can be made that can be detrimental and dangerous to the animal populations. What can go wrong?

1. It is important that a sufficient number of animals are tagged. For this simulation, it is suggested that 100 red beans be used. If the jar being used is very large, it will be

Mathematical Connections:
Data collection and analysis, statistics, percentage of difference

Other Curricular Connections:
Poetry, environmental science

Concepts:
Students will:

- Participate in a capture–recapture data collection simulation
- Use ratio and proportion to understand how large populations can be "counted"
- Predict the larger population using a representative sample
- Find the mean in each sample
- Use percentage of difference to analyze the reliability of this data collection process

Materials Needed:

- A jar filled with an unknown quantity of white beans and 100 red beans
- Worksheet "How Many Bears in the Forest—Capture–Recapture?" for each student
- Overhead transparency of "Class Data Table"
- Calculators

necessary to increase this number. To save time, you may tell the students how many red beans there are in the population.

2. During each capture, it is very important that the tagged "bears" (red beans) be allowed to disperse into the general population—a vigorous shaking will disperse them. For this reason, the beans should be housed in a container that is large enough to accommodate both the red and the white beans.

3. It is important to have a sufficient number of recaptures. While in the real world these might be very expensive, if there are too few the results may be inaccurate.

The student direction sheet discusses sampling and provides directions for the simulation. This can be read with the class. After students understand the data collection process, explain that the class is going to conduct a capture–recapture simulation using red and white beans; the red beans represent bears in the forest that have been tagged. The sum of the white beans (untagged bears) and red beans represent the entire population of bears.

Assessment:

1. Journal question: "Explain how capture-recapture data collection can be used to make predictions. Give a real-world example (other than the one done in class) of how this type of data collection might be used."

Capture-Recapture: How Many Beans?

The poem "Keepin' Count," in Shel Silverstein book *Falling Up*, is about a little boy trying to count the number of flies in a jar. The boy counts to 3 million and 7 when a baby fly is born—and he has to start all over again! Even though there is sometimes an exact amount of *things* in a "jar" (a forest, a lake, or an ocean), we can't find an exact amount by counting.

How do you think scientists might *count* the number of brown bears there are in a forest? Although there are a certain number, they cannot be counted by ordinary means either. So, they use a type of data collection called "sampling"—it involves capturing the bears, tagging them, and then releasing them back into the wild. This is called "capture-recapture" because the original number of bears are first captured and tagged, then a series of recapturing is done, and a ratio is set up of tagged to untagged bears. Scientists assume that there will be a similar ratio of tagged to untagged bears in the greater population. We are going to use this type of sampling technique and conduct a simulation of a capture-recapture experiment to estimate how many beans in this jar.

Follow these steps:

1. Count the red beans—these represent all of the tagged bears.

2. Now *release* them into the jar (forest) and mix them well.

3. Scoop out a sample. This is called a "recapture." Record your data on the Class Data Table.

4. Now release them back into the jar (our forest). Repeat this 20 times.

5. Calculate the mean number of red-tagged bears recaptured.

6. Calculate the mean of each of the captures (total number in the scoop).

7. Set up the following proportion:

$$\frac{\text{Mean \# of red beans in each recapture}}{\text{Mean \# of total beans in each recapture}} = \frac{\text{Total \# of red beans in the jar}}{\text{Total \# of all beans in the jar}}$$

8. Solve for "*x*." By counting the beans in the jar, you can see how accurate you were!

Capture-Recapture: How Many Beans?

Class Data Table

TRIAL	Tagged (Red Beans)	Total Beans in Sample (All of the Beans Including Red)
1		
2		
3		
4		
5		
6		
7		
8		
9		
10		
11		
12		
13		
14		
15		
16		
17		
18		
19		
20		
MEAN		

Find the following answers using the data in the Class Data Table.

Total mean number of white and red beans (calculated from the capture–recapture sampling):

Total of all the beans (obtained by taking an actual count of all of the red and white beans in the jar):

What is the difference between the total obtained from sampling and the actual count?

To mathematically determine how accurate this sampling was, we can find the percentage of difference:

$$\text{Percentage of difference} = \frac{\text{amount of difference}}{\text{actual number in jar}} \times 100$$

Percentage of difference: _____

LOOKING FOR MATH IN POETRY: FLAVORS OF ICE CREAM

Teacher's Planning Information

Background Information and Procedures:

The poem "Ice Cream Stop," in Shel Silverstein's book *Falling Up,* tells of a circus train that stops at an ice cream stand that serves 52 flavors of ice cream. Related to this poem, students are asked to problem-solve all the combinations of possible two-flavor ice cream cones by looking for patterns, listing all of the possibilities, using problem-solving skills (including elimination and collection of organized data), and drawing conclusions. Since there are actually 1,326 different combinations of two-flavor ice cream cones that can be made using 52 flavors of ice cream, the activity starts out with a smaller number and, using a table to help students see a pattern, has them progress up to 10. Suppose two of the flavors are chocolate and vanilla—a two-flavored cone would contain one scoop of chocolate and one of vanilla. It would not matter if the chocolate flavor was on the top or the bottom. Also, a cone cannot contain two scoops of the same flavor.

While there is a formula that advanced mathematics students can use to calculate the number of combinations, it is often memorized and they do not see the pattern that develops as the number of flavors is increased.

The formula used to calculate the number of combinations is: $C_r = \dfrac{n!}{(n-r)! * r!}$

So if there were six flavors of ice cream and we wanted two-flavor cones:

$$_6C_2 = \frac{6!}{(6-2)! * 2!} = \frac{6 \cdot 5 \cdot 4 \cdot 3 \cdot 2 \cdot 1}{(4 \cdot 3 \cdot 2 \cdot 1) * 2 \cdot 1} = \frac{6 \cdot 5}{2} = 15$$

This strategy is included as background information and is not recommended as a possible solution for middle school students. Using tables, listing possible combinations, and exploring developing patterns are much more appropriate for most students of this level.

Mathematical Connections:
Combinations, numerical patterns, figurate numbers, algebra, problem solving

Other Curricular Connections:
Poetry

Concepts:
Students will:

- Predict, calculate, and then generalize the number of two-flavor combinations that can be made from 10 flavors of ice cream
- Discover a number pattern
- Problem-solve strategies to extrapolate that pattern

Materials Needed:
- Worksheet of "Flavors of Ice Cream" for each pair of students
- Calculators

Students can begin the lesson by reading the poem. Ask, "If each animal has only a single-scoop cone, how many different cones can there be? What happens if they decide to get two-flavor cones? Will they still be able to get 52 different cones?" Be sure students understand that the order that the flavors appear in the cone is not important. Have students estimate how many different cones are possible. Then group them in pairs and give them the worksheet, "Flavors of Ice Cream." After each group has completed their sheet, discuss their results, what answers they got, and how they solved the problem. Many different strategies can be used to solve this type of problem—matrixes, tree diagrams, or an organized table are three possibilities. On the worksheet, a table is used to help students organize their solutions and find a pattern. The final column of this table asks students to solve for the 52 flavors listed in Silverstein's poem.

Let's look at some of the strategies students might use when solving for six flavors of ice cream:

An organized table

1,2	1,3	1,4	1,5	1,6
2,3	2,4	2,5	2,6	
3,4	3,5	3,6		
4,5	4,6			
5,6				

Solution: $5 + 4 + 3 + 2 + 1 = 15$ combinations of two-flavor ice cream cones

Using a matrix

The numbers represent the six flavors, and the shaded areas represent either cones that have only one flavor or those that are duplicates of the same two flavors.

	1	2	3	4	5	6
1	1,1	1,2	1,3	1,4	1,5	1,6
2	2,1	2,2	2,3	2,4	2,5	2,6
3	3,1	3,2	3,3	3,4	3,5	3,6
4	4,1	4,2	4,3	4,4	4,5	4,6
5	5,1	5,2	5,3	5,4	5,5	5,6
6	6,1	6,2	6,3	6,4	6,5	6,6

A tree diagram

A visual representation of an organized list.

	2 ___	1,2
	3 ___	1,3
1	4 ___	1,4
	5 ___	1,5
	6 ___	1,6
	3 ___	2,3
2	4 ___	2,4
	5 ___	2,5
	6 ___	2,6
	4 ___	3,4
3	5 ___	3,5
	6 ___	3,6
4	5 ___	4,5
	6 ___	4,6
5	6 ___	5,6

Assessment:

1. Problem-solving strategies shown on student worksheet

2. Journal question: "There are eight students in row 1. How many ways can students be paired up to work on a project? Be sure to explain how you solved this problem (perhaps you might use a diagram or table).

Flavors of Ice Cream—Selected Answers:

Number of Flavors	1	2	3	4	5	6	7	8	9	10	20	52
Number of Two-Flavor, Double-Scoop Cones	0	1	3	6	10	15	21	28	36	45	190	1326

Because the flavors are taken two at a time, the numbers formed by this pattern are triangular numbers. A formula can be used to find any triangular number: $\dfrac{t \cdot (t-1)}{2}$ where t = the term

In this problem, t represents the number of flavors sold. Encourage students to find a formula that can be used for any number of flavors. Remember to encourage different versions of the same solution.

Flavors of Ice Cream

Name _____

Date _____ Class _____

An ice cream parlor serves 10 different flavors of ice cream. You have a class of 25 students. Can each person in the class get a two-flavor, double-scoop cone with no two students getting the same two flavors?

Before you start working on this problem, make a guess! How many different two-flavor, double-scoop cones can be made if the store has 10 different flavors of ice cream?

Sometimes it is easier to solve a simpler problem or to organize our work so that patterns develop. Let's look at an easier problem first: What if there were only two or three different flavors?

Directions: This type of problem can be solved in many different ways. Work with your partner to develop a problem-solving strategy and complete this table. Use the space provided to explain how you solved the problem.

Number of Flavors	1	2	3	4	5	6	7	8	9	10	20	52
Number of Two-Flavor, Double-Scoop Cones	0	1	3									

How we solved this problem:

LOOKING FOR MATH IN POETRY: OVERDUE BOOK FINES

Teacher's Planning Information

Background Information and Procedures:

Shel Silverstein's poem "Overdues" in *A Light in the Attic* tells the tale of a man who has a library book that is 42 years overdue. This activity assumes that his library has no maximum fine and so he is responsible to pay the fine for each day of the 42 years it has been in his possession!

The mathematics of this problem is fairly simple and students should be able to do it without the use of calculators. After students calculate the fine at 10¢/day, they are asked to calculate it based upon the fine imposed by their school (or local library.)

> **Mathematical Connections:**
> Computation, conversions, mental math, problem solving
>
> **Other Curricular Connections:**
> Poetry
>
> **Concepts:**
> Students will:
>
> - Convert years to days
> - Calculate the fine per day × number of days
>
> **Materials Needed:**
> - Worksheet of "Overdue Book Fines" for each student
> - Calculators (if necessary)

Assessment:

1. Correct solution on worksheet "Overdue Book Fines"

2. Journal question: "Suppose the maximum fine at your local library for an overdue book is the cost of the book. The book you have neglected to return costs $12.95 and the fine is 15¢/day. After how many days would you be better off paying for the book than paying the fine? Explain how you got your answer." [12.95 ÷ .15 is a little bit over 86 days]

Overdue Book Fines—Selected Answers:

The book has been overdue for 15,330 days (365 × 42). If the fine is 10¢/day, then the fine is $1,533.00.

Overdue Book Fines

Name _____

Date _____ Class _____

In Shel Silverstein's poem "Overdues," a man is concerned because his library book is 42 years overdue! This creates an interesting math problem—how much money would be due on this book if the fine is 10¢ each day (and the library does not have a maximum amount the fine can be)?

Directions:

1. Calculate how much a fine of 10¢ per day would be if the book is 42 years overdue. Be sure to express your answer using appropriate units of measure.

2. Research how much your school library fines are and how much it would cost in fines if you waited 42 years to return an overdue book.

How we solved this problem:

TRAVELING TO LILLIPUT: HOW LITTLE WERE THE LILLIPUTIANS?

Teacher's Planning Information

Background Information and Procedures:

Jonathan Swift's *Gulliver's Travels* is a powerful satire of society that combines the tale of a fantastic voyage with a serious philosophical and social message. The book can help integrate topics of interest in social studies, language arts, and mathematics classes.

Swift was born in Dublin, Ireland, on November 30, 1667. Ordained as an Anglican priest, Swift wrote *Gulliver's Travels* while serving as dean of St. Patrick's Cathedral in Dublin. Published in 1726, the book's satire was directed at the inequities of the English Whigs, and Swift became a hero in his native Ireland.

In social studies, students can examine how social satire has been used to foster change. Are political cartoons a form of twentieth-century satire? How are they used to bring our attention to social issues?

In mathematics, *Gulliver's Travels* provides the basis for a problem-solving activity that asks students to draw a Lilliputian, knowing only that they are 6 inches tall! Using measuring, averages, and conversion ratios, students find the length of a Lilliputian's arm, the size of its head, the length from its head to its waist, the size of its hands, and the length of its legs. Using these measurements, they can draw a full-size portrait of this little person.

This activity highlights Gulliver's stop at the land of Lilliput. His second voyage takes him to the land of Brobdingnag, where the people are 60 feet tall—120 times the size of a Lilliputian! In this land of giants, grass grows to a height of 20 feet, a man's stride is 10 yards long, and a small cup holds about 3 gallons of liquid. These statistics could be the beginning of interesting follow-up activities that focus on length and volume.

Mathematical Connections:
Measurement, data collection and analysis, scale drawing, ratio and proportion

Other Curricular Connections:
Literature and social studies

Concepts:
Students will:

- Measure their height and use it in a conversion ratio
- Use the conversion ratio to approximate the size of the body parts of a Lilliputian
- Draw a Lilliputian to scale

Materials Needed:
- Tape measures, rulers, or yard sticks
- Copy of student worksheet "How Little Were the Lilliputians?" for each group
- Copy of "How Little Were the Lilliputians? Page 3" for each student
- Colored pencils, crayons, or markers

With the students, read the excerpt from *Gulliver's Travels* on the "How Little Were the Lilliputians?" student worksheet. Discuss that Gulliver had washed up on the beach and was captured by tiny people called Lilliputians. Gulliver tells of this experience while tied to the ground with thousands of little stakes and rope. The Lilliputians are walking on his body when he awakes. Ask the students, "If a person is only 6 inches tall, how big do you think his head would be? His arms? His legs?"

Explain what the conversion ratio represents and how it can be used to find the size of a Lilliputian's body parts. If a person is 60 inches tall (or 5 feet), the ratio 6:60 computes to 1/10 or 0.1. If all of the student ratios are averaged to the nearest tenth, the conversions become easy and more understandable. Give students time to collect their data and draw their Lilliputian. Pictures can be displayed around the room.

Assessment:

1. Successful completion of student data collection sheets

2. Journal question: "Explain how your group used the conversion ratio to problem-solve the size of the Lilliputian. Can you think of any other applications where conversion ratios might be used?"

Traveling to Lilliput: How Little Were the Lilliputians?—Selected Answers:

Answers will vary depending on measurements taken by groups. But a decimal ratio between a child who is 5 feet tall (60 inches) and a Lilliputian (6 inches) is rounded to the nearest tenth. In this example, it rounds to .01 or 1/10. This is a very "friendly number" for students to work with.

How Little Were the Lilliputians? Page 1

Name _____

Date _____ Class _____

Gulliver's Travels by Jonathan Swift is a fantastic tale of the voyages of Lemuel Gulliver, a ship's surgeon who is shipwrecked. When he washes up on the beach, the residents of Lilliput become very alarmed by this giant because they are only 6 inches tall. Swift describes Gulliver's reactions in the following way:

> I felt something alive moving on my left leg, which advancing gently forward over my chest, came almost up to my chin; when bending my eyes downwards as much as I could, I perceived it to be a human creature not six inches high, with a bow and arrow in his hands, and a quiver at his back. . . . I roared so loud that they all ran back in a fright; and some of them, as I was afterwards told, were hurt with the falls they got by leaping from my sides upon the ground.

It would be interesting to figure out how long a Lilliputian's arms were, how long their fingers were, or how big their heads were! We can do this by using a conversion ratio computed by using their heights and our heights!

$$\text{Conversion ratio} = \frac{\text{Lilliputians Height (6 in.)}}{\text{Average Group Height (in.)}}$$

Using the group data collection sheet "How Little Were the Lilliputians? Page 2," your group will:

1. Carefully measure the height of each group member and enter it on the table.

2. Convert your height to a fraction and decimal ratio.

3. Find the mean decimal ratio for your group. Round that number to the nearest tenth.

How Little Were the Lilliputians? Page 2

Finding Our Group's Conversion Ratio

Name	Height in Inches	Ratio = $\dfrac{6\text{ in.}}{\text{Your height}}$	Decimal (Rounded to 0.1)
MEAN			

Using Our Conversion Ratio to Estimate the Height of the Lilliputian

Measurement	Person 1	Person 2	Person 3	Person 4	Mean	Mean × Conversion Ratio	Size of Lilliputian
Length of arm (shoulder to tip of finger)							
Width of head (ear to ear)							
Length of head (top of head to chin)							
Length of torso (top of head to waist)							
Length of hand (wrist to end of fingers)							
Length of leg (hip joint to floor)							

Use these measurements to decide on the scale you will use to draw a Lilliputian.

How Little Were the Lilliputians? Page 3

Name _____

Date _____ Class _____

Use this graph to draw a picture of a Lilliputian. Use the size calculated by your group. Each square is 1/4 inch.

A MILLION IS A VERY BIG NUMBER: SPENDING $1,000,000

Teacher's Planning Information

Background Information and Procedures:

In *The Toothpaste Millionaire* by Jean Merrill, sixth grader Rufus Mayflower becomes upset that a little tube of toothpaste costs 79¢—he knows that all you need to make toothpaste is bicarbonate of soda and water! He can make a gallon of toothpaste for the same cost as a 6-inch tube. With the help of some of his friends and his math teacher, by the time he's in eighth grade, he has made $1,000,000! But how long will it take to spend $1 million? That is the basis of this problem. To extend the problem, students can be asked to design a spreadsheet and answer the question, "How long will it take to spend $1 billion?"

The two spreadsheets on the next page show that while it takes 20 days to spend $1 million, it takes only another 10 days to spend 1,000 times as much money! $(1,000,000,000 = 1000 \times 1,000,000)$

Mathematical Connections:
Computation, problem solving

Other Curricular Connections:
Literature

Concepts:
Students will:

- Compute the number of days it takes to spend $1 million
- As an extension activity, design a spreadsheet to compute the number of days it takes to spend $1 billion

Materials Needed:
- Student worksheet "Spending $1,000,000" for each student
- Calculators
- Computers with spreadsheet program (if necessary)

Assessment:

1. Correct calculations on student worksheet

2. Journal question, "If I told you that the distance between Atlanta and Chicago is 44,342,000 inches, you would not have any idea how far apart these cities actually are because inches are not a reasonable unit of measure to use when describing large distances. Convert 44,342,000 inches to miles to find the distance between these two cities." [Answer: 44,342,000 in. ÷ 12 in. 3,695,167 ft. ÷ 5,280 ft. 700 mi]

Day	Amount Spent	Total Amount Spent	Day	Amount Spent	Total Amount Spent
1	$1	$1			
2	$2	$3	1	1	1
3	$4	$7	2	2	=B6+C5
4	$8	$15	=A6+1	=B6*2	=B7+C6
5	$16	$31	=A7+1	=B7*2	=B8+C7
6	$32	$63	=A8+1	=B8*2	=B9+C8
7	$64	$127	=A9+1	=B9*2	=B10+C9
8	$128	$255	=A10+1	=B10*2	=B11+C10
9	$256	$511	=A11+1	=B11*2	=B12+C11
10	$512	$1,023	=A12+1	=B12*2	=B13+C12
11	$1,024	$2,047	=A13+1	=B13*2	=B14+C13
12	$2,048	$4,095	=A14+1	=B14*2	=B15+C14
13	$4,096	$8,191	=A15+1	=B15*2	=B16+C15
14	$8,192	$16,383	=A16+1	=B16*2	=B17+C16
15	$16,384	$32,767	=A17+1	=B17*2	=B18+C17
16	$32,768	$65,535	=A18+1	=B18*2	=B19+C18
17	$65,536	$131,071	=A19+1	=B19*2	=B20+C19
18	$131,072	$262,143	=A20+1	=B20*2	=B21+C20
19	$262,144	$524,287	=A21+1	=B21*2	=B22+C21
20	$524,288	$1,048,575	=A22+1	=B22*2	=B23+C22
21	$1,048,576	$2,097,151	=A23+1	=B23*2	=B24+C23
22	$2,097,152	$4,194,303	=A24+1	=B24*2	=B25+C24
23	$4,194,304	$8,388,607	=A25+1	=B25*2	=B26+C25
24	$8,388,608	$16,777,215	=A26+1	=B26*2	=B27+C26
25	$16,777,216	$33,554,431	=A27+1	=B27*2	=B28+C27
26	$33,554,432	$67,108,863	=A28+1	=B28*2	=B29+C28
27	$67,108,864	$134,217,727	=A29+1	=B29*2	=B30+C29
28	$134,217,728	$268,435,455	=A30+1	=B30*2	=B31+C30
29	$268,435,456	$536,870,911			
30	$536,870,912	$1,073,741,823			

Spending $1,000,000— Selected Answers:

On the 19th day, Rufus has spent $524,287. On the 20th day, he has spent over $1,000,000.

Day	Amount spent today	Total amount spent
1	$1	$1
2	2	3
3	4	7
4	8	15
5	16	31
6	32	63
7	64	127
8	128	255
9	256	511
10	512	1,023
11	1,024	2,047
12	2,048	4,095
13	4,096	8,191
14	8,192	16,383
15	16,384	32,767
16	32,768	65,535
17	65,536	131,071
18	131,072	262,143
19	262,144	524,287
20	524,288	1,048,575

Spending $1,000,000

Name _____

Date _____ Class _____

In Jean Merrill's *The Toothpaste Millionaire,* Rufus Mayflower becomes a millionaire by making better and less expensive toothpaste. Being a curious boy, Rufus decides to spend his money in the following way: One the first day after he becomes a millionaire he will spend $1.00; on the second day, he will spend $2.00; on the third day, he will spend $4.00; on the fourth day, he will spend $8.00, and so on. He wonders how many days it will take for him to spend the entire $1,000,000.

First estimate how many days you think it will take him: _____ Then use the table on the next page to help you solve this problem. You might need to add on some days! A few days of spending are done to get you started.

Day	Amount spent today	Total amount spent
1	$1	$1
2	$2	$3
3	$4	
4		
5		
6		
7		
8		
9		
10		
11		
12		
13		
14		
15		
16		
17		
18		
19		
20		
21		
22		
23		
24		
25		

A MILLION IS A VERY BIG NUMBER: HOW BIG A BOX DO WE NEED FOR 1,000,000 PENNIES?

Teacher's Planning Information

Background Information and Procedures:

This activity can be used with David M. Schwartz's book, *If You Made a Million.*

In this book, a little girl earns a penny, then a nickel (worth five pennies), then a dime (worth two nickels or 10 pennies), and so on, until she earns $1,000,000 (a stack of pennies 95 miles high! At the back of the book, Schwartz has suggestions about interest rates, banking, income tax, and more.

Allow students to work with a partner for this activity. Each pair of students will need copies of the student worksheets, "Open-Top Box" and "How Big a Box Do We Need for 1,000,000 Pennies?" Before they begin, ask them if they can visualize the size of a box that will hold a million pennies. Give them time to discuss this problem and find real-world examples of boxes that might be big enough.

After students cut out and construct the open-top box, give each group 20 pennies to help them solve the problem.

When all of the groups have entered their data on the Class Data Table, ask each group how they calculated the number of pennies their 3 × 3 × 1½-inch box would hold and how they decided on the dimensions of their box.

Mathematical Connections:
Area, volume, computation, problem solving

Other Curricular Connections:
Literature

Concepts:
Students will:

- Cut out and construct an open-top box
- Estimate the dimensions and volume of a container large enough to hold 1 million pennies

Materials Needed:

- Copy of worksheet "An Open-Top Box" for each pair of students
- Copy of worksheet "How Big a Box Do We Need for 1,000,000 Pennies?" for each pair of students
- Calculators
- Scissors
- Scotch tape
- Overhead transparency of Class Data Table
- Twenty pennies for each pair of students

Assessment:

1. Accuracy of calculations and measurements on student worksheet

2. Journal question: "A stack of 16 pennies is approximately 1 inch tall. About how many miles high would a stack of 1 million pennies be? Be sure to show how you solved each step of this problem." [Ans.: $1,000,000 \div 16 = 62,500$ in. $\div 12$ 5,208 ft. or just under one mile]

How Big a Box Do We Need for 1,000,000 Pennies?—Selected Answers:

The value of 1 million pennies is $10,000.

The dimensions of a box that will hold 1 million pennies: Answers will vary. On the Web site http://www.kokogiak.com/megapenny/six.asp possible dimensions of 4 ft. × 5 ft. × 1 ft. are given for 1,003,776 pennies.

How Big a Box Do We Need for 1,000,000 Pennies?

Name _____

Date _____ Class _____

How big a container do you think you would need to hold 1,000,000 pennies? Would they fit in a very large carton? In a box the size of a refrigerator? Talk to your group and write down your estimate of how big a container you think you would need: _____

How much are 1,000,000 pennies worth using appropriate units? _____

Now we are going to cut out and fold an open-top box following the directions on the next page. You and your partner will use this box to help you solve this problem.

Use this space to describe the strategies you used to solve this problem and be sure to show your work:

We think 1,000,000 pennies might fit in a box with the following dimensions:

_____

Its volume would be: _____

Share your measurements and conclusions with the rest of the class on the Class Data Table.

An Open-Top Box

Cut on the solid lines and fold on the dotted lines. Then tape the flaps inside and use this box to help you estimate the size box you would need to hold 1,000,000 pennies.

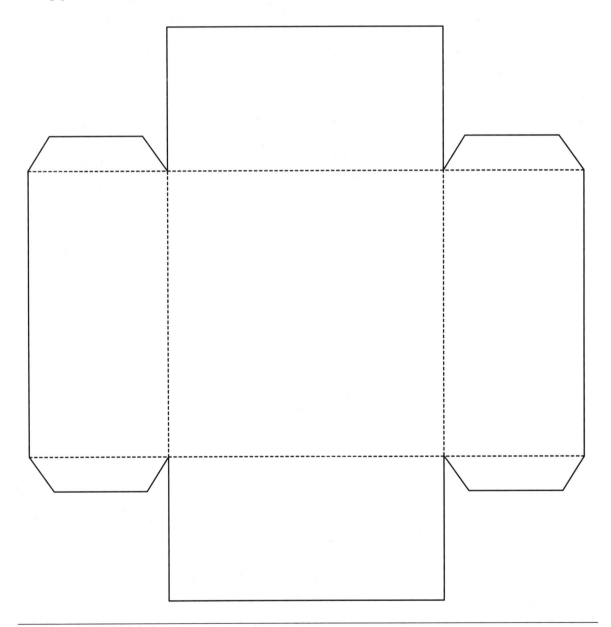

How Big a Box Do We Need for 1,000,000 Pennies?

Class Data Table

Group	Number of Pennies Our $3 \times 3 \times 1\frac{1}{2}$ Box Will Hold	Dimensions of Our Million-Penny Container	Volume of Our Million-Penny Container

A MILLION IS A VERY BIG NUMBER: A MILLION STARS

Teacher's Planning Information

Background Information and Procedures:

David Schwartz's book *How Much Is a Million?* has seven pages that are filled with tiny little stars. He tells us that there are 100,000 stars and if we take this seven-page journey 10 times, we will have over a million stars. The activity "A Million Stars" is adapted from this idea.

Students, working in pairs, are given a sheet of stars (asterisks). The sheet has 55 stars in each row and 40 rows for a total of 2,200 stars. Students are asked to find the number of stars on the sheet and then solve three problems: (1) How many sheets of paper will they need to have 1 million stars? (2) How much will these sheets of paper weigh? and (3) Do they have enough sheets of paper to wallpaper their classroom with star paper?

The answers to these questions are in the "Selected Answers" section.

An extension activity might be to ask students to answer these same questions, but this time they are to accumulate 1 billion stars. Each of their measurements would be one thousand times the size calculated for 1 million stars.

Assessment:

1. Correct answers on the student worksheet

2. Journal question: "A dollar bill is 0.0043 inches thick. You would need approximately 233 one-dollar bills stacked one on top of the other to have a stack that is 1 inch high. How high would a stack of 1,000,000 one-dollar bills be?" [Answer: approximately 348 feet]

Mathematical Connections:
Computation, measurement, area, problem solving

Other Curricular Connections:
Literature

Concepts:
Students will:

- Calculate the number of sheets of paper needed to have 1 million stars
- Estimate the surface area of their classroom
- Ascertain if they can wallpaper their classroom using the number of sheets of paper in the million star problem

Materials Needed:
- Student worksheet "A Million Stars" and sheet of stars for each pair of students
- Scale
- Yardsticks
- Calculators
- One ream of paper

A Million Stars—Selected Answers:

1. There are 55×40 stars on the paper or 2,200 stars.

2. To accumulate 1,000,000 stars, we need to have approximately 834 sheets of paper.

3. One ream (500 sheets of paper) weighs 5 pounds. Set up a ratio:

$$\frac{5 \text{ lb.}}{500 \text{ sheets}} = \frac{x \text{ lb.}}{834 \text{ sheets}}$$

$x = 8.34$ lb., or about 8-1/3 pounds.

4. For the purposes of showing a solution to this problem, we will assume that the classroom is 15 ft. wide x 15 ft. long x 8 ft. high. One wall that is $15' \times 8'$ is $180" \times 96"$—its area is 17,280 sq. in. Each sheet of 8 1/2" $\times$ 11" paper has an area of 93.5 sq. in. $17,280 \div 93.5 = 185$; so 185 sheets would be needed to cover one wall completely in a $15 \times 15 \times 8$ room. To find an exact answer, the students will need to have the exact measurements of their classroom. The method of calculating the answer would be the same as that shown above.

A Million Stars

Name _____

Date _____ Class _____

David Schwartz's book *How Much Is a Million?* has seven pages that are filled with 100,000 tiny stars. He tells us that if we have 10 times the number of pages of stars, we would pass 1,000,000 stars. A million of anything seems to be a very large amount!!

For this activity, you will work with a partner to solve these problems:

1. Count the number of stars on your page of stars. How many are there? _____

2. Calculate how many sheets of paper you would need to have 1 million stars.

   We would need _____ sheets of paper.

3. How much will these many sheets of paper weigh? _____

4. Do we have enough sheets to wallpaper our classroom with star paper?

   Why or why not? _____

Use the space below to show how you solved each of these problems—be specific!

How we solved these problems:

ADDITIONAL READING

Merrill, J. (1972). *The toothpaste millionaire.* New York: Sandpiper.

A delightful story about a creative and persistent sixth grader who, along with his friends and teacher, makes a million dollars by selling a better and cheaper toothpaste.

Paulos, J. A. (2001). *Innumeracy: Mathematical illiteracy and its consequences.* New York: Hill and Wang.

Paulos examines the problems well-educated Americans have with mathematical principles, in particular large numbers and probability, and the costs (both economically and socially) of our innumeracy.

Schwartz, D. M. (1989). *If you made a million.* New York: Mulberry.

This book relates a picture story about a little girl who earns a penny, then a nickel (worth five pennies), then a dime (worth two nickels or 10 pennies), until she earns $1,000,000 (a stack of pennies 95 miles high!). This book is used in the activity "How Big a Box Do We Need for 1,000,000 Pennies?" to help students visualize the volume of 1 million pennies.

Silverstein, S. (1981). *A light in the attic.* New York: HarperCollins.

One of Silverstein's collections of poems. This one contains the poem "Overdues" that is used in this chapter.

Silverstein, S. (1996). *Falling Up.* New York: HarperCollins.

One of Silverstein's collections of poems. This one contains the poems "Ice Cream Stop" and "Keepin' Count" that are used in this chapter.

INTERNET WEB SITES

http://shelsilverstein.com/indexSite.html

The opening page of a most creative Web site! If high bandwidth is used, a very clever cartoon introduction is shown, followed by a page that allows viewers to choose from "For Kids Only!" "What's New," "Shel's Books," "About Shel," and "Ideas for Teachers & Parents."

http://www.pbs.org/teachersource/mathline/lessonplans/msmp/somethingfishy/some thingfishy_procedure.shtm

A PBS lesson discusses an environmental issue using a capture–recapture strategy with fish.

http://www.jaffebros.com/lee/gulliver/contents.html

An online version of Swift's book *Gulliver's Travels.*

http://www.kokogiak.com/megapenny/default.asp

This Web site helps students visualize very large numbers by showing what 1 to 1 quintillion pennies might look like. The site includes their dollar value, their dimensions, and the area they would cover.

http://www.vendian.org/envelope/dir0/grain_feel.html

This site explains large numbers using salt—from one grain to a trillion grains. A tablespoon holds 100,000 grains of salt, and 1,000,000,000 grains of salt will fill a bathtub!

http://ga.water.usgs.gov/edu/mgd.html

How much is a million gallons of water? This Web site gives some interesting information—including that it would fill 200 fifty-gallon bathtubs!

Resource A

Alternatives to Traditional Assessment

When instruction engages students as active participants rather than passive learners, teachers need to look beyond traditional assessment strategies and move toward a more multifaceted assessment that accurately describes where the student is. Performance assessment, sometimes referred to as *authentic assessment,* requires students to perform tasks, create products, or problem-solve multi-step, nontraditional mathematics tasks. Such tasks cannot always be "graded" as right or wrong; they cannot always be evaluated using traditional methods.

The activities and projects in *Making Math Connections* have investigations that engage the students in thought-provoking, meaningful mathematics; make students active participants in the learning process; and have activities and projects that allow students to work together and share ideas and strategies. What are some ways that teachers can assess learning when using nontraditional lessons?

Performance assessment may take the form of journals, student products, completion of tasks, or open-ended problems. Students may be asked to present their ideas or conclusions in verbal or written form. Good assessment is designed to be compatible with the particular mathematical task. It encourages students to use strategies that are appropriate for the activity, helps foster persistence, encourages thinking in a variety of styles, and allows for multiple avenues to approach a problem (making it accessible to more students).

USING RUBRICS

Rubrics are scoring scales used to evaluate a student's performance based on levels of degrees of mastery. A good rubric looks at all of the components of the problem and has concrete criteria to help assess student performance. An activity or problem might contain all or some of these elements: performing computation, making charts or graphs, explaining procedures or results in written form, or participating in open-ended problem solving. Each of these components needs to be assessed in a different way.

Computation or mathematics mechanics can be evaluated using paper-and-pencil tests, but a rubric can be used to assess not only the correctness of the answer but also the degree to which it was accomplished. Here is an example of a rubric that might be used to assess the accuracy of the mathematics mechanics:

	4	3	2	1	0
Accuracy of mathematics mechanics	Has completed the problem with no math errors	Has completed the problem with no major or serious flaws but with one or two math errors	Has completed the problem with some major or serious flaws and with one or two math errors	Has completed the problem with many major or serious flaws and with math errors	Has not completed the project

By using this type of rubric, teachers can credit students for what they have gotten correct and indicate areas that need improvement. What are the characteristics and design of a good rubric? First, the criteria align with the curriculum and method of instruction. Once you know what it is that you want to teach and what you want your students to learn, you are ready to develop your assessment criteria. Think of your students' progress on a continuum from least developed to most developed, and have a clear understanding of the performance levels between these two extremes. Be sure to share the rubric with students so they are aware of the purpose of the lesson and important skills and concepts.

OBSERVATION OF STUDENTS

While students are working in groups and the teacher is visiting groups, student observations can be an informal way to assess student progress. Many of the lessons and projects require the active involvement of students. Observe how well the students work in their groups and what each student contributes to the final product. This type of observation provides a clear indication of the students' understanding.

Interviewing Students

As you walk around observing students, stop and question them: Can you explain to me what you're doing? Why do you think that happened? Did anyone in the group have another idea of how this might be done?

Journal Questions for Each Lesson

Journal writing is probably the most effective method of using writing to teach mathematics (Neil, 1996). Students learn to use vocabulary in a problem-solving setting and make sense of arithmetic, algebra, and geometry by describing their strategies in their own words. Countryman (1992) states, "Good journals give evidence of students using a wide variety of thinking skills . . . providing a teacher with considerably more information about how students are approaching and using mathematical concepts than most formal assignments can offer"(p. 32). Each activity and project in *Making Math Connections* contains at least one journal question.

Resource B

Design Your Own Lessons

GETTING STARTED

Knowledge is not isolated into discrete, neat subject areas. As research indicates, students will not learn unless they can make connections and construct knowledge from previously learned information. How do you get started? Historical information or knowledge of scientific principles can help your students make "real-world" connections. Current events can be used to make the activity relevant—using national elections and the electoral college or the cost of gasoline and gas mileage of automobiles shows students how we "use math every day." Meet with members of your team and consider teaching units that interrelate during the same school term. Perhaps quilting can be taught in the mathematics class, while the social studies teacher teaches about colonial America and the language arts teacher has students read a novel related to this same time period, such as *Sign of the Beaver* by Elizabeth George Speare.

CURRICULUM-WRITING TIME

Textbooks often have a section that relates a mathematics skill or concept to "math in the real world." While the authors may relate exponents to astronomy, very often the problem is very low skilled, such as "Convert 100,000,000 to a number in scientific notation." Many interesting investigations can get students actively involved in very large numbers and vast distances. For example, the National Optical Astronomy Observatory Web site, http://www.noao.edu/education/peppercorn/pcmain.html, gets the math teacher started on a wonderful activity that describes not only distances between planets but the relative size of planets. Use *Making Math Connections* to help you get started on designing your own lessons.

FLEXIBILITY OF TIME

While lessons that utilize real-world applications generally take more time than pages in a textbook, the mathematics that students learn is well worth not only the effort but also the time involved. Research shows that when students make connections (NCTM, 2000), they understand how mathematical ideas interconnect and can then build one on another to produce a coherent whole.

THE FIRST STEPS

Carefully examine the lesson you want to work with:

1. What are the major skills and concepts in the lesson?

2. What applications can you apply to these skills and concepts?

DESIGNING THE PROGRAM

You are now ready to delineate the components of the activity. You can use the following Teacher's Planning Information form to help define the activity. It is sometimes easier to work backwards—write up the activity first and then analyze it to find the mathematical connections, curricular connections, materials needed, and so forth. Use one of the Venn diagrams to make connections less ambiguous—which concepts and skills do the disciplines have in common and which are unique?

DEFINING ASSESSMENT

When mathematics is taught and learned in a nontraditional way, it is sometimes necessary to consider alternatives to traditional assessment strategies. Authentic assessment of your project will require alternatives to paper-and-pencil tests. Review the suggestions made in "Resource A: Alternatives to Traditional Assessment."

FORMS TO ORGANIZE THE ACTIVITY

Venn diagrams and a teacher's planning page follow to help with organization.

TWO-SUBJECT VENN

The two-subject Venn is used to describe connections between mathematics and one other discipline. This can be used when the mathematics and science teachers want to integrate the teaching of density, or the social studies and mathematics teachers want to integrate integers, map reading, and time zones.

MATHEMATICS _____

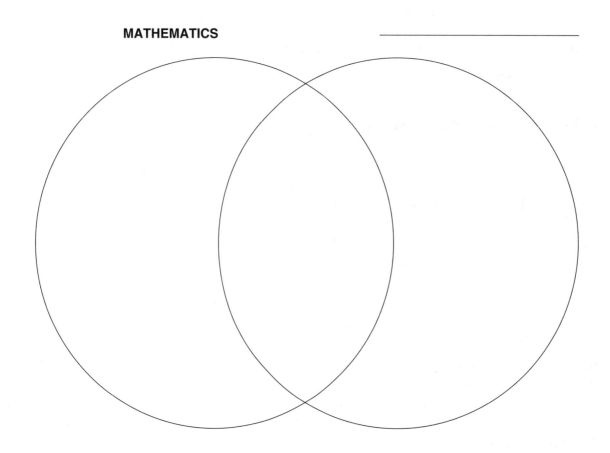

TOPIC: _____

_____

THREE-SUBJECT VENN

The three-subject Venn is used to show connections among three disciplines. Perhaps in mathematics, students are working on transformational geometry and tessellations, in social studies they are exploring Islamic history and the tiling at the Alhambra, while in art they are investigating the work of M. C. Escher.

MATHEMATICS _____

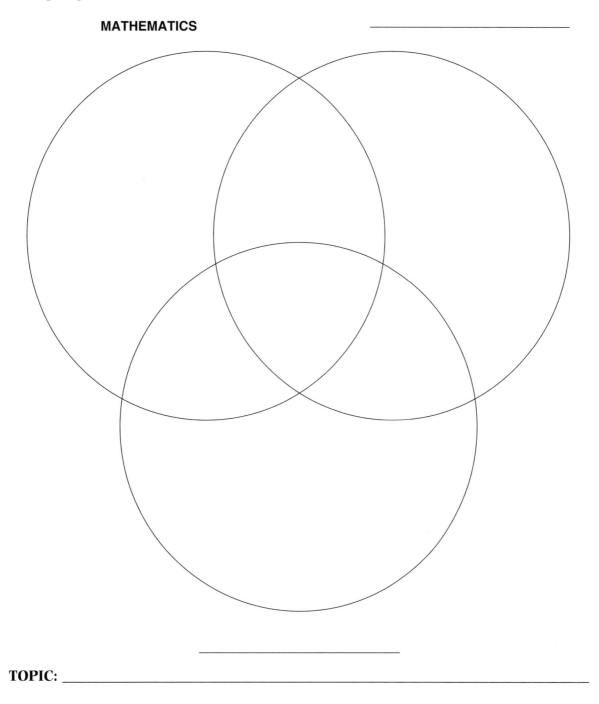

_____

TOPIC: _____

_____

_____

FOUR-SUBJECT VENN

When four curricular areas are interrelated, this model will help define overlapping skills and concepts, as well as the skills and concepts that are unique to each discipline.

MATHEMATICS _____

_____   _____

TOPIC: _____

_____

TEACHER'S PLANNING INFORMATION

Mathematical Connections:

Other Curricular Connections:

Concepts: Students will:

Materials Needed:

Background Information and Procedures:

Assessment:

1. Journal question:

2.

3.

Selected Answers:

Additional Readings and Internet Web Sites:

Bibliography

American Association for the Advancement of Science. (1989). *Science for all Americans: Project 2061.* New York: Oxford University Press.

Countryman, J. (1992). *Writing to learn: Strategies that work.* Portsmouth, NH: Heinemann.

deLange, J. (1996). Using and applying mathematics in education. In A. J. Bishop, et al. (Eds.), *International handbook of mathematics education,* pp. 49–97.

Freudenthal, H. (1991). *Revisiting mathematics education.* China lectures. Dordrecht, The Netherlands: Kluwer.

Johnson, D. R. (1982). *Every minute counts: Making your math class work.* Palo Alto, CA: Dale Seymour.

Lochner, J. L. (1971). *The world of M. C. Escher.* New York: Abrams.

National Council of Teachers of Mathematics [NCTM]. (2000). *Principles and standards of school mathematics.* Reston, VA: NCTM.

National Council of Teachers of Mathematics. (2000). *Mathematics assessment: A practical handbook for grades 6–8* (W. S. Bush & S. Leinwand, Eds.). Reston, VA: NCTM.

National Research Council. (1989). *Everybody counts: A report to the nation on the future of mathematics education.* Washington, DC: National Academy Press.

National Research Council. (2001). *Adding it up: Helping children learn mathematics* (J. Kilpatrick, J. Swafford, & B. Findell, Eds.). Washington, DC: National Academy Press.

Neil, M. S. (1996). *Mathematics the write way: Activities for every elementary classroom.* Larchmont, NY: Eye on Education.

Pappas, T. (1995). *The music of reason.* San Carlos, CA: Wide World Publishing/Tetra.

Zulkardi & Nieveen, N. (2001). CASCADE-IMEI: *Web site support for student teachers learning Realistic Mathematics Education (RME) in Indonesia.* Paper presented at the ICTMT5 conference, Klagenfurt, Austria, August 6–9, 2001.

INTERNET REFERENCES

http://www.noaa.gov

Site of the National Oceanic & Atmospheric Administration. It contains up-to-date information about a variety of weather-related phenomena and natural disasters including air quality, droughts, floods, hurricanes, lightning, tornadoes, tsunamis, and volcanoes.

http://neic.usgs.gov

The Web site of the National Earthquake Information Center (NEIC). The job of the NEIC is to determine the location and size of all destructive earthquakes worldwide and to immediately disseminate this information to concerned national and international agencies, scientists, and the general public via this Web site.

http://earthquake.usgs.gov/recenteqs

An interactive site that allows students to view earthquakes that occurred in the United States from one hour ago to one week ago. By clicking on a particular earthquake site, students learn where it occurred, when it occurred, its magnitude, and more. It is an interesting way for students to learn how many earthquakes occur that we are unaware of because they are not very powerful.

**CORWIN
PRESS**

The Corwin Press logo—a raven striding across an open book—represents the union of courage and learning. Corwin Press is committed to improving education for all learners by publishing books and other professional development resources for those serving the field of PreK–12 education. By providing practical, hands-on materials, Corwin Press continues to carry out the promise of its motto: **"Helping Educators Do Their Work Better."**